BAMBOO

BAMBOO

A Material for Landscape and Garden Design

Jan Oprins
Harry van Trier

Photographs: Hugo Maertens

Birkhäuser – Publishers for Architecture
Basel • Berlin • Boston

Contents

Preface

Reading this bamboo book may have serious consequences...

I grew up in a rural environment. As a child I was fascinated by nature. Collecting and growing plants was my hobby. My studies in school also went in that direction. Later my hobby became my profession. I developed a broad interest and became fascinated by the search for new markets and developments.

Bamboo changed my life, helped me expand my horizons. I learned to look beyond Belgium and Europe. Ultimately I ended up in the countries from which bamboo came. I discovered that they have thousands of years of experience with bamboo and that it can be used in countless ways. It is used in the garden and in the kitchen, in buildings and in furniture; pulp and paper, woven baskets and handbags are made from it. In short, the possibilities are endless.

During my trips through bamboo-land, I made many friends. Meetings of the various bamboo societies became like real annual family reunions. We shared love and pain, exchanged news, told each other about new developments, made plans, dreamed and reflected together. Everyone was valued for his specific knowledge and contribution.

Starting to cultivate this magnificent plant from nature is an enormous challenge; we want to grow and propagate it. For this, we made our first steps into the enthralling world of biotechnology. Fascinated by bamboo as we are, we search and collect data, develop theories, experiment. Despite setbacks and disappointments, we feel a compulsion to go on and search for improvement, always retaining a respect for nature, which still has so many secrets for us.

Our objective is to grow – with adequate effort – an attractive product in the right pot and in the right soil. The economic aspect is also important: we intend to offer an affordable product. The marketing must work properly. We want to develop a reputation for quality. Logistics are also increasingly important for us. We are even already exporting bamboos to China.

Selecting and developing new bamboos into successful consumer plants is and remains a great challenge. This foreign plant deserves a place in our Western culture, as a house plant or garden plant, as a green screen, barrier or hedge. The fanciful growth and winter green fit wonderfully into modern garden design.

And the future? I see three possibilities for bamboo: first as an ornamental plant, second as a plant for development projects, and third in industrial cultivation that produces biomass. What other plant has so much to offer?

The dream that all this hard work will contribute to producing an improved environment is stronger than the economic interests, which are necessary in order to keep everything running.

Bamboo cultivation is still in its infancy in Europe. Around the end of the 19th century there were three bamboo pioneers active on the European continent. Eugène Mazel realised his dream of a bamboo forest in the neighbourhood of Nîmes. This became the basis for the Bambouseraie de Prafrance. Another collection was planted in Baden-Baden, in the German Black Forest. It contributed to stimulating Wolfgang Eberts's interest in bamboo. In Belgium, near Mons, Jean Houzeau de Lehaie assembled a collection of bamboo that was extraordinary for its time. This remarkable man was also the publisher of the first bamboo journal in Europe. These somewhat forgotten pioneers laid the foundation for the current interest in this exceptional plant.

This book offers you a selection of the possibilities for bamboo in Western society. Specialists of all sorts from the world of bamboo have contributed their visions. They share their knowledge and experience with you, and with everyone who has an interest in the subject. Anyone who has not yet caught bamboo fever is warned. This book could have serious consequences for you.

p. 8-9: *Phyllostachys nigra* 'Boryana' on the edge of a pond in the Bokrijk Arboretum in Belgium

The Plant Kingdom

About bamboo

Bamboos are grasses. In other words, they belong to the large and important family of the *Poaceae* (previously termed *Graminae*). This family comprises a very large number of economically important plants. One need think only of the cereal grasses, but there are many others in addition. We can say with confidence that without the *Poaceae* the form of our lives as human beings would be entirely different. That is true for us as Europeans, and even more the case if we look at the world as a whole. *Poaceae* include about 650 families with about 10,000 species. The bamboos are grouped in a separate subfamily, the *Bambusoideae*.

Grasses are among what botanists call monocotyledonous plants: their seeds have only one seed lobe, in contrast to what are termed dicotyledons, whose seeds have two seed lobes. The seed lobes are structures which contain a reserve of food for the sprouting plant. In the case of the cereals, these food reserves are generally what we eat as human beings (together with that other reserve structure, the endosperm). Monocotyledonous plants have a number of other characteristics in common that distinguish them from dicotyledons. For instance, on the leaves we generally find several veins running parallel with each other, and internally the structure of the stalk is entirely different. Monocotyledonous plants are therefore not a source of real wood, in the botanical sense of that word. When there is a trunk, as in the case of the palms, the wood from it cannot be sawn up into boards, and one finds no annual growth rings. A grass stalk is usually hollow, although it can sometimes be full. Generally speaking, the buds, points where leaves and lateral branches are situated, appear as swellings on the stalk. These buds are also termed nodes. The sections between the nodes are then internodes. In the otherwise hollow stalks, the nodes are full.

Origin and source

Grasses have been around for a very long time, but because they do not produce wood cells, they have left behind few fossil remains. Thus we must deduce the existence of grasses from their use. We can see from the fossils of extinct animals that some of them have the grinding teeth that are characteristic of herbivores. This shows we can assume that grasses already existed at the beginning of the Cretaceous period, running from 135 to about 65 million years ago. The grasses of that age were unlike those today. Apparently they were herbaceous plants in tropical forests. A small, wide-leafed species from the tropical rainforest which still exists today, *Streptochaeta spicata*, reminds us of such primitive grasses.

In contrast to what was believed previously, we know from modern research that bamboos are not so primitive. They apparently split off from the real grasses about 30 to 40 million years ago.

There are no wild bamboos in Europe today. But that does not mean that there never were any. Rather recently fossil bamboos have been found in France and other places, more specifically in Andance, south of Lyon. But bamboos reached their widest distribution and diversity in Asia and South America. What is more – and at first sight would

Young shoots of *Phyllostachys aureosulcata* 'Aureocaulis' turn a gorgeous red in a sunny environment

Phyllostachys vivax with young shoots that will grow into stems 6 to 7 cm in diameter

seem most amazing – is that the bamboos of these so widely separated continents are related. DNA research indicates, for instance, that the North American *Arundinaria gigantea* is related to the Chinese species *Pseudosasa amabilis*. Is this an argument supporting the existence of Gondwana, the ancient super-continent?

In our gardens we are most familiar with the Asian group, numerous species of which come from China. It is unlikely that all of the varieties which are to be found in that vast land have already been discovered. Yet we cannot say that China has the largest diversity in bamboos. Botanists are increasingly realising that the greatest wealth in species and varieties must be sought in Central and South America. Views differ on the number of species of bamboo there are – and there is probably also a large number of species still awaiting discovery. Therefore there is little sense in giving a figure here. We will however emphasise that the natural distribution of bamboos is enormous, from about 46 degrees northern latitude to around 47 degrees southern latitude. The region in which bamboos can be cultivated is still wider. There are examples of bamboos being raised in the northern hemisphere above the sixtieth parallel. Bamboos thus display a considerable diversityand capacity to adapt themselves.

Bamboo in its natural environment in Yangshuo, China

The structure of bamboo

One does not need to be a botanist to know that part of a bamboo plant is underground, and part above ground. It is thus logical to consider these parts separately, starting with the part that is most often forgotten by the majority of garden enthusiasts.

Root systems are particularly important for most plants, but they also often cause most of the problems in a garden. That is certainly the case for bamboo. Many gardeners have come to regret that they ever planted bamboos.

'They just run rampant!' is a frequently heard complaint. And indeed, a species such as *Sasaella ramosa* is better not planted in a private garden, unless you want to have a quarrel with your neighbours. But that doesn't have to be the case with all bamboos.

The terminology applied to root systems is a rather complex matter. With regard to bamboos we will speak of rhizomes. These are not really roots, but underground stems. The actual roots, which bamboos necessarily also have, will not concern us here. For our purposes it is sufficient to distinguish between two types of bamboos: species where the roots form a clump and species where the

(Above) *Fargesia* 'Jiu':
left, clump-forming root system;
right, adult plant.
(Below) *Phyllostachys nigra* 'Boryana':
left, runner-forming root system;
right, adult plant.
p. 18: Contrasting green stripes on a yellow
background are characteristic of the stems of
Phyllostachys vivax 'Aureocaulis'.
Height, 6 to 8 m; stem thickness, 4 to 6 cm
p. 19: Belly-shaped internodes are characteristic
of the slow-growing *Pseudosasa japonica*
'Tsutsumiana'. Height, 2 to 3 m

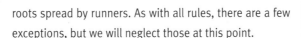

roots spread by runners. As with all rules, there are a few exceptions, but we will neglect those at this point.

The first group, those with the clump-forming root systems, is the one which can most easily be kept under control in a garden. The rootstocks (or rhizomes, and thus really underground stems) have short segments, which are reflected in the close-growing, erect stems above the ground, and thus the formation of a clump. Each growing point of the rhizome forms a node, which produces roots and a culm. Then the rhizome grows a bit further, producing a new section of rhizome, and the whole process repeats itself. Ultimately this results in a compact underground network of rhizomes, generally coupled with a thick bunch of above-ground stalks. In the case of the second type, the species with running roots, the rootstock looks like a stem growing just under the ground. The roots and subsidiary nodes growing from the underground nodes will each develop into an above-ground stalk. We often find roots on the underground portion of these culms. Species with a root system like this can very rapidly take over a rather large area. These rootstocks are not only longer but also thinner than in the bamboos with clump-forming roots.

The terms which are used for this, and thus refer to the manner in which the rhizomes branch, are sympodial and monopodial, respectively. With sympodial plants it is the side axes which predominate, with monopodial plants it is the principal axis. In the literature one can find still other terms which, for the sake of completeness, we will briefly mention here. Pachymorphic is a word that is used to indicate types with short rhizomes, or actually, one should say, rhizomes with short, thick segments. Leptomorphic is then used for rhizomes with long, thin segments.

Fargesia angustissima propagated by tissue culture, juvenile plant

In practice, pachymorphic types, roughly speaking, correspond with sympodial types, and leptomorphic types are almost equivalent to monopodial types. If we look at the way bamboos grow above the ground, then we find that they are sometimes divided into caespitose species (which one can more or less equate with pachymorphic types) and diffuse-growing species (which again to a great extent correspond with leptomorphic rhizome growth). The categorizations are indeed complicated. For gardeners it is primarily the above-ground growth which will determine how bamboo is used in the garden.

Sympodial bamboos are generally easy to keep under control in a garden. Dig a deep and wide channel around the clump with a spade, and the problem is usually solved. Or dig in a rhizome barrier when they are planted. The latter is an absolute necessity for bamboos with a monopodial or leptomorphic root system. Be careful that the rhizome barrier is installed properly – that is to say, at the right depth, depending on the type of bamboo being planted, and with a sufficient number of centimetres above the ground, and with a sufficient overlap at the ends. In this way you can keep the bamboo in its own place, and if there is still a stem which manages to escape, you can take prompt action with your spade to solve the problem.

Above the ground, bamboo consists of culms (or stems, if you prefer) and leaves. It is this above-ground section that contains the ornamental value for which bamboo is cultivated.

Culms. The culms of bamboos are comprised of a main stem with filled joints (nodes) and hollow sections in between (internodes), and a number of side branches, which often appear only after the second season. The main stem consists of alternating full and hollow sections (with the exception of a genus like *Chusquea*, in which the whole culm has a full structure). The full parts are relatively small, but they are very important: the nodes are not much more than partitions, but it is from these points that leaves and axillary nodes grow. The external characteristics of the hollow internodes account for much of the ornamental value of bamboos, for these stem sections are often beautifully coloured, sometimes multi-coloured.

Each node can grow into a side branch with leaves. This occurs primarily through upward growth, in which the nodes move out from one another, like sections of a telescope. The speed with which this happens can be surprising. It is because of this that it is said that you can see a bamboo grow.

Culm leaves. Around each node – where the active growth of the plant is taking place and thus where the chance of damage is greatest – there is a structure that protects the young sprout. This is what is called the culm leaf or bract.

Striking stem sheaths on *Fargesia robusta* (Campbell). Height, 3 to 5 m

Sasaella glabra 'Albostriata' has superb yellow-white lengthwise stripes on its leaves. Height, 1 to 2 m

The use of rhizome barriers is definitely advised with bamboos with runner-forming root systems

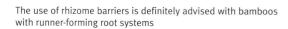

It is very important for the plant's growth, and under no circumstances should it be removed prematurely. Sometimes it drops off after it has fulfilled its purpose, and sometimes it continues to hang dead on the stem. The characteristics of the bract are a good aid in the identification of bamboos. The structure of a bract is rather peculiar. On the one hand it looks like a normal leaf, on the

Thanks to its origins (the Kuril Islands, north of Hokkaido), *Sasa kurilensis* is suitable for the coldest places in the garden. Height, 1 to 2 m

other the proportions are entirely different. A culm leaf consists of a large section that surrounds the stem, called the culm sheath. On top of this we find a smaller, pointed section, the leaf blade. Situated on the upper side of the culm sheath we find two ears, called auricles, and sometimes also a tongue or ligula.

Real leaves. The leaves that are formed on the side branches, termed real leaves, have a structure similar to that of the culm leaves, but here the leaf blade is much larger and more important, because it is this part of the leaf which is chiefly responsible for photosynthesis or chlorophyll activity. The leaf blade is separated from the leaf sheath (to be compared with the culm sheath of a culm leaf) by a pseudo-leaf stalk. This looks like a leaf stalk, but is different in structure.

This is not the only quality through which bamboo leaves are different from grass leaves. In addition, they are often multi-coloured, but just by their shape, grouping and profusion alone they contribute to the ornamental value of the plant. In principle bamboos remain green through the winter, although they often shed some of their leaves when circumstances are less favourable. If we hold a bamboo leaf up to the light, we can easily see the net structure of the ribs. A main rib runs over the length of the whole leaf, an extension of the leaf stalk. This is supported by a number of secondary veins parallel to it, which are connected to one another by cross-veins.

Flowers. We cannot speak about the structure of bamboo without devoting at least a few words to the flowers. As garden lovers, we would rather not see the flowers, for they do not contribute anything of importance to the aesthetics of the bamboo, and often lead to the plant dying back. That is true at least for the above-ground parts of pachymorphic or clump-growing types. We are however speaking here about a full bloom, and not stalks blooming here and there in a group. It is sometimes possible to keep blooming bamboos alive, but this demands constant care and attention. Often it is easier to replace a flowering plant by a non-flowering example.

Flowering in bamboo – here in *Fargesia nitida* – is a phenomenon still not entirely understood

The leaves of *Pleioblastus variegatus* have irregular white stripes. Height, 0.5 to 1.2 m

The internal beauty of the bamboo stalk

Bamboo is often valued for its elegant appearance. This esteem is based on the outward characteristics, such as the colour of the culm, and the form and size of the plant. Almost no one is concerned with the interior structures and functions which are the basis for the living stalk. Their functional performance is even more important than in trees. The bamboo shoot develops its large stalk – and biomass – in the surprisingly short period of several months. But after that all the interior structures must continue to function for the whole life of the stem. Trees have the advantage that they develop a new growth ring each year, with new cells taking over for any possible damage to the older cells. Equally fascinating is the fact that the growing bamboo shoot has no leaves to provide it with energy by means of photosynthesis or the action of chlorophyll.

A seedling of a tree develops its first leaves within several days so that it can produce energy for itself. The growing bamboo shoot however contains an enormous amount of carbohydrates as its source of energy. These carbohydrates are carried from the rootstock and the older stems by a very efficient transport system. Moreover, the provision of energy for the rapidly growing stems corresponds with the creation of technically perfect forms with superior strength characteristics. The many wonders of bamboo cannot be understood without an insight into its anatomical structure.

In contrast to wood, bamboo stalks display a rather simple anatomical structure without any notable differences among the many sorts. On the outside the epidermis or cuticle provides protection against loss of moisture and physical damage. On the hollow interior a specially adapted layer of cells also provides a boundary layer. About 60%

Left: Three-dimensional view of stem structures with vascular bundles embedded in parenchymatous cell tissue

Center:
Trachea surrounded by parenchymatous cell tissue

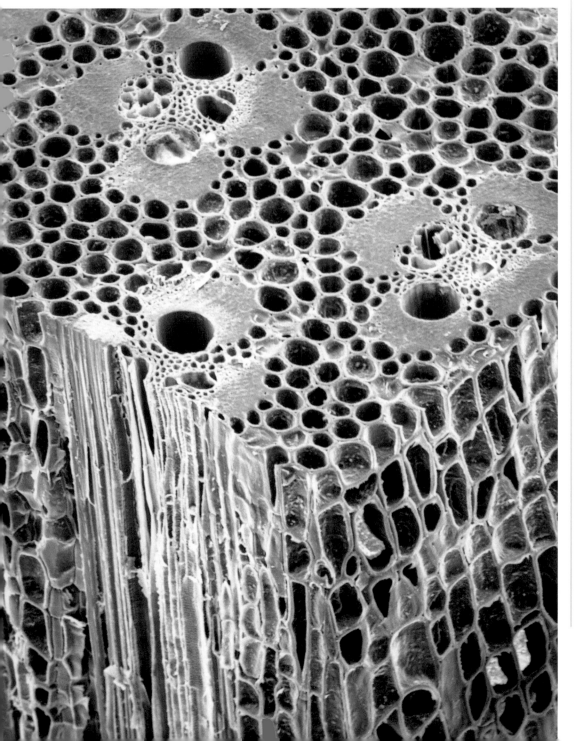

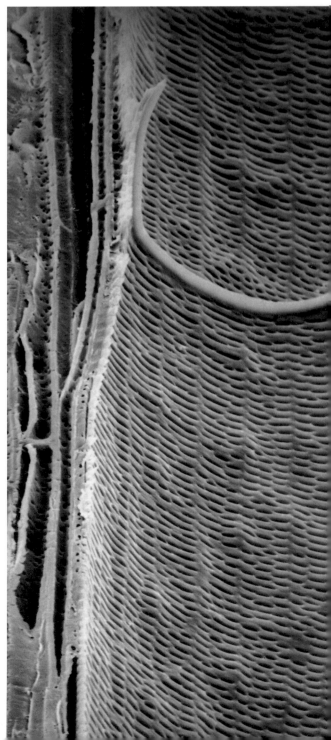

of the stem is made up of parenchymatous cells which serve a storage function, 35% of fibre for strength, and 10% of conductive tissue for water (tracheae) and sugars (sieve tubes). Two large tracheae and the sieve tubes form the vascular bundles, which in turn are surrounded by the fibres which account for the plant's strength. Large tropical bamboos, such as *Bambusa* and *Dendrocalamus*, have separate fibre bundles for additional support. The darker-coloured vascular bundles are embedded in tissue made up of parenchymatous cells. The tracheae and sieve tubes run perfectly vertical in the stem, branching only at the nodes. A trachea is surrounded by parenchymatous cells, fed by smaller openings that facilitate the exchange of water among the cells. A cross-section of a stem reveals a great number of vascular bundles, differing in form and number. The vascular bundles are smaller and larger in number on the outside; toward the inside of the stem they are larger, but fewer in number.

Around the vascular bundles on the inside one finds primarily filling tissue (parenchymatous cells) and vascular cells, while on the outside there are many more fibres to be found, which provide strength. The number of fibres increases as one moves from the bottom of the plant up, and the filling tissue diminishes in proportion.

The fibres comprise about 50-70% of the weight of the stem tissue. They are about 2 to 3 mm long – thus longer than the fibres in hardwood, but shorter than those of the conifers. The walls of fibre cells are characterised by a clearly layered structure. Up to ten layers develop during the first three years. The wall is constructed of microfibres which run in different directions from layer to layer. The stalks mature through the thickening of the fibre cell walls. Their structure can be compared with that of plywood, in which three thin layers of wood with their grain running in different directions are stronger than one

Layers in the fibre cell wall with microfibres running in different directions

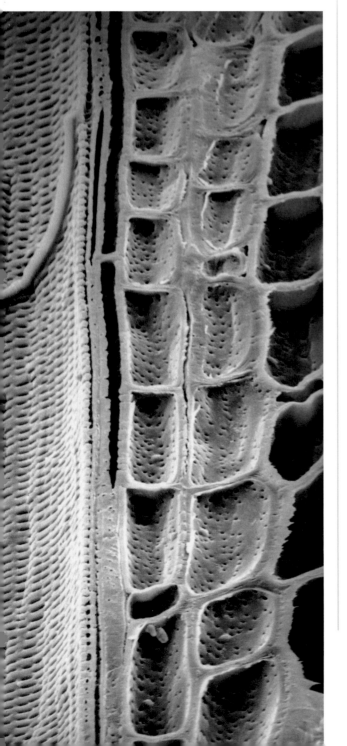

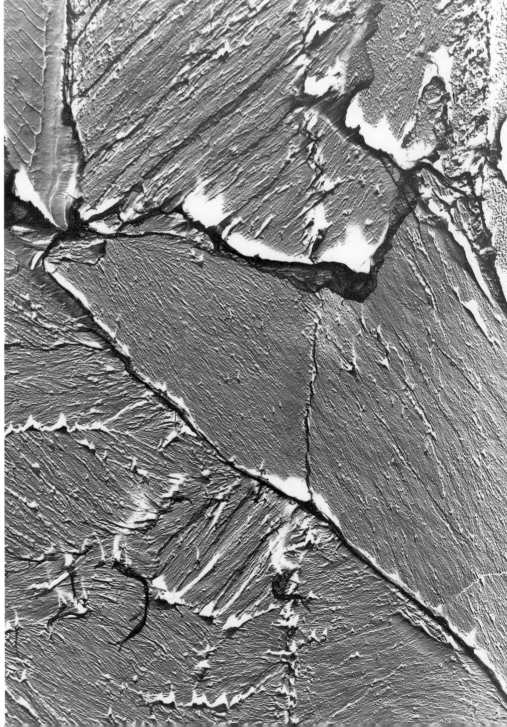

Cross-section of a fibre cell wall consisting of various sheets

single layer with its grain running in one direction would be. And as a further comparison: fibres in trees have only three layers in their cell walls!

The parenchymatous cells store the energy for the development of the expected new shoots. Before new shoots begin to grow, these cells fill themselves with grains of starch. During their transport from the rootstock and older stems, these grains of starch are temporarily transformed into sugars, which can be dissolved in water. Although the parenchymatous cells are rather short, their walls are also comprised of several layers with differing arrangements in their building blocks.

The rootstocks or rhizomes are the underground part of the bamboo stalk. They grow and branch out entirely underground, and at their nodes these rhizomes have fine roots that absorb nutrients from the soil. New nodes form on the rhizomes that will grow up into new shoots.

The rhizomes also serve to stabilise the whole plant, and function for the storage of energy for growth and under-

ground expansion. Therefore the tissue contains even more parenchymatous cells, because these serve as storage spaces, and more fibres for strength. The air canals in the rhizomes of some species of bamboo which grow in damp soil are also worth mentioning; these canals allow for air circulation in the rootstock.

Wounds to the plant can lead to structural changes. If a stem is damaged, the admission of air must be avoided, because air bubbles can cause stoppages in the tracheae. The parenchymatous cells around the wound respond to block the tracheae by forming slimy substances or balloon-like bulges. Similar reactions occur when the stem is harvested. This therefore influences the drying process (giving off water) and protection (admission of moisture).

The structure of the bamboo stem is thus a very effective system for transport, storage and strength, and is the basis for the numerous uses of bamboo.

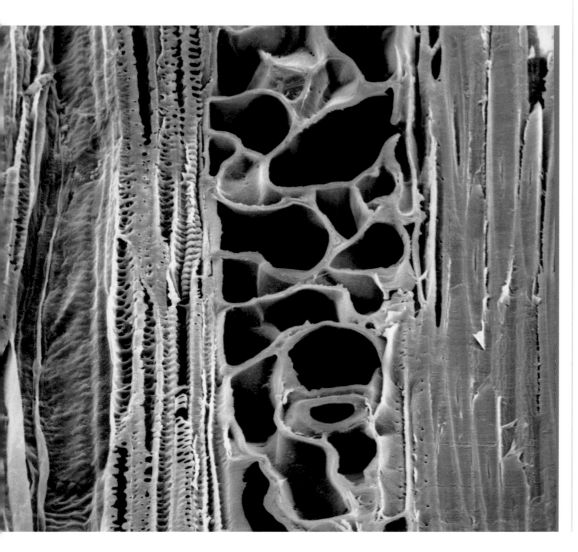

Stoppage in a trachea to prevent the spread of air

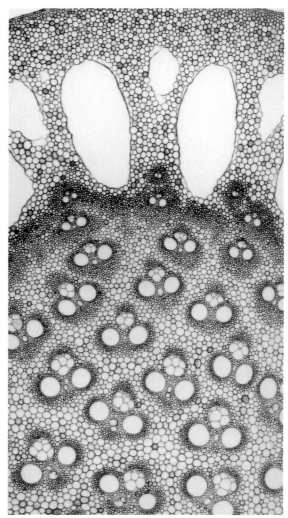

Rhizome with air canals and a fibrous ring

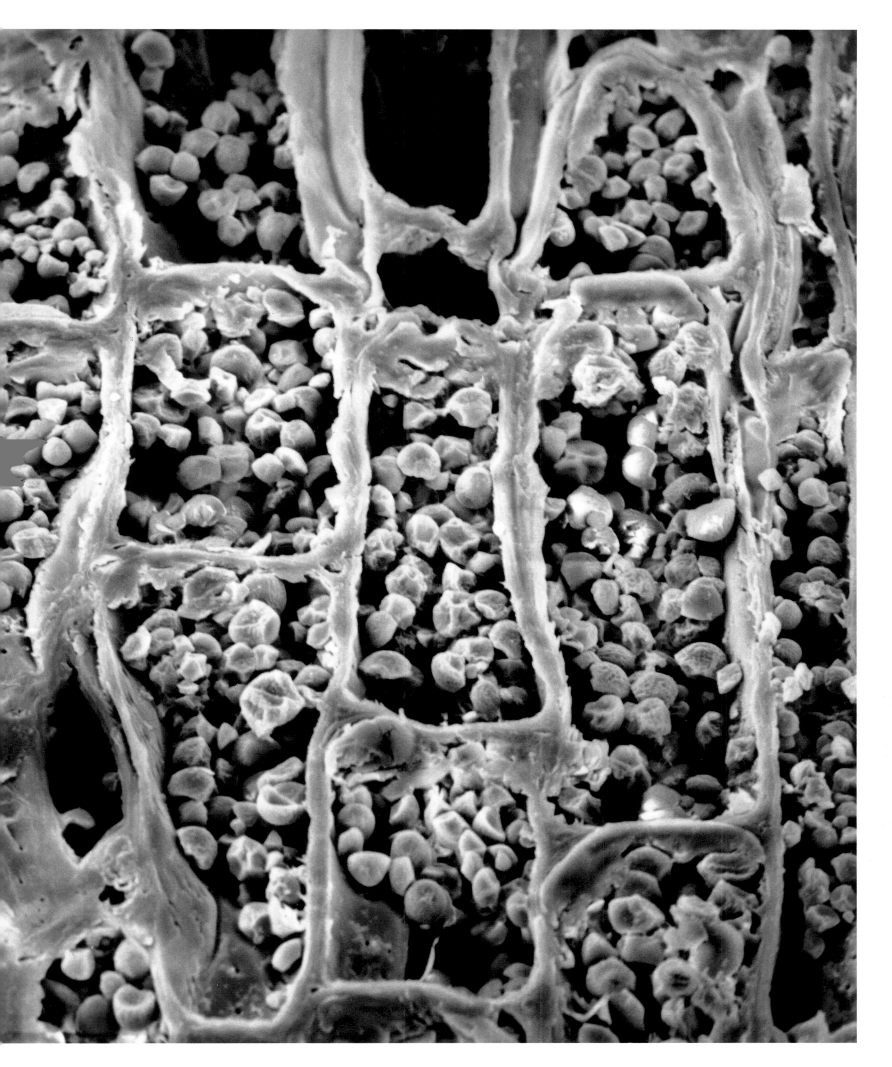

Parenchymatous cells filled with grains of starch

Propagation

Overgrowth along the banks of the Li River, Yangshuo, China

Fargesia 'Rufa' is particularly well suited for use in large containers on a terrace or patio

The fascination for bamboo

As the Asian continent became accessible in the 18th and 19th centuries, Europeans were overwhelmed not only by the technology and culture, but also by Asia's natural environments, its fauna and flora. In the 19th century massive numbers of new plants were imported into Europe. Plants such as apple trees, roses and rhododendrons have their origins in the temperate regions of Asia, as do countless other garden plants.

One of the most fascinating and impressive plants was undoubtedly bamboo. In the Asian cultures, bamboo is totally intertwined with daily life. Everyday utensils, bamboo houses, pens and paper of bamboo: these are but a few of the countless applications for which the plant was used in the Far East. In India, Europeans found giant tropical bamboos 30 m high. In China and Japan, plant collectors encountered hardy bamboos with magnificent stem colours and great variation in plant shape and leaf forms.

Thus it was not long before the first bamboos were imported into Europe as exotic specialities. Around the beginning of

the 19th century bamboos were introduced into European ornamental plant cultivation. Initially there were only a handful of species, very spectacular for their time, such as the golden bamboo (*Phyllostachys aurea*) and black bamboo (*Phyllostachys nigra*) from China. Gradually more and more sorts were imported as ornamental plants. At the beginning of the 20th century there were more than 500 sorts of bamboo in Europe, primarily in the hands of specialised collectors. However, of these only about fifty were really suitable for use as decorative plants in the gardens and public parks of Western Europe. These species are sufficiently hardy to withstand European winters and have great ornamental value in our gardens. Bamboo can be used as a solitary plant, for hedges and screens, for planting in beds and as a potted plant.

Hardy ornamental bamboos can be subdivided into three general groups, a division that also corresponds to their taxonomic division. For our gardens we can speak of the fascination of *Phyllostachys*, the grace of *Fargesia*, and the adaptability of *Sasa*. The first group – the *Phyllostachys* group – are large bamboos between 4 and 15 m tall, belonging to the *Phyllostachys* and *Semiarundinaria* families. The stem colours in these sorts are spectacular, varying from yellow through green to totally black. These bamboos are used in our gardens as solitary plants and for high screens. There is one important exception, namely *Shibataea*, the lucky bamboos, which grow only 1.5 m high, but belong botanically to this same group of bamboos with creeping rhizomes or rootstocks. *Shibataea* are therefore used for planting in beds, or for lower hedges. The second group are somewhat lower bamboos with pachymorphic rhizomes, with a height of 2 to 4 m. The *Fargesia* group includes species from the mountainous regions of south-west China, among them *Fargesia*, *Thamnocalamus* and *Yushania*. These bamboos are used as hedges and as potted plants. The third group, the *Sasa* group, embraces lower-growing and middle-height bamboos (from 0.5 to 3 m tall) from Japan and China. These are creeping, low-growing bamboos with names like *Pseudosasa*, *Pleioblastus*, *Sasa* and *Arundinaria*. They form impenetrable hedges and screens, and the lower sorts are suitable for low hedges, ground cover or planting in beds.

Until recently, as ornamental plants bamboos were relatively expensive, and the more special their type, the more the plants cost in the trade. The reason for this was clear. From the 1980s, when interest in bamboo as an ornamental plant began to rise in Europe, until several years ago, the demand vastly exceeded the supply. There simply were not enough bamboos in supply, and thus the prices remained high. Bamboos were, and still are, propagated

Sasaella ramosa in the Kalmthout Arboretum, Belgium: suitable as ground vegetation in parks or mixed woods. Height, 1 to 1.5 m

Bamboo seeds make its relationship with grasses and grain clear

chiefly by separating one plant into multiple sections. This is a time-consuming method, and it takes years before you get thousands of descendants from one single plant.

If one wishes to introduce a new species in this manner, it takes between five and ten years before one has sufficient numbers for sale. Since our garden production is driven by the continual introduction of new species, by selection or improvement, bamboo threatened to be forgotten. Moreover, highly sought-after sorts such as black bamboo hardly ever appeared in stock, and were expensive. Therefore an intensive search began for a better method of propagation.

Bamboo can be propagated by various 'classic' methods, by seed, by cuttings, and by splitting. With seed, people make use of the generative phase of the plant, with blossoms, flowers and seed formation. Cuttings and division are vegetal propagation techniques. However, none of these classic methods is as successful as micropropagation by means of tissue culture, a technique which was perfected in Europe.

Propagation by seed

Bamboos are grasses, and their seeds strongly resemble grains of wheat, although there are several tropical bamboos in which the seed is encased in a fleshy fruit. While a number of tropical bamboos can be propagated by means of seed, for most of them this method is unusable. In order to understand why, some knowledge about the flowering of bamboos is necessary. There are a very large number of different flowering patterns among bamboos, such as annual flowering, mass flowering and cyclical flowering. Mass flowering is the most familiar form, in which especially tropical bamboos flower simultaneously over large areas. Obviously, this appeals to the imagination. In the late 1970s bamboo bloomed massively in southwest China, in the territory of the giant panda. There were a number of causes for this flowering, such as the increasing deforestation in this region, but the giant panda was threatened by the disappearance of its main food source.

The giant panda – the symbol par excellence for species under threat – eats primarily bamboo shoots, many kilos a day. A species related to the blooming bamboos in the panda's territory, *Fargesia murieliae*, came into bloom massively in our region after 1993, and in the cultivation of ornamental plants that flowering brought forth a new generation. These are only two examples for the major consequences blossoming can have especially for the local population.

Whole bamboo forests die off when the huge numbers of seeds produced at the time by the old generation trigger off the growth of a complete new generation of plants. Certain tropical bamboos bloom in cycles, for instance of forty to fifty years. Some species of *Phyllostachys* can have a cycle of eighty years or more.

The causes of this simultaneous flowering are as yet unknown, and florescence among bamboos remains one of the greatest mysteries in the plant kingdom. Mass flowering appeals to the imagination, and contributes to the shaping of myths about florescence among bamboos. However, by far the most bamboos do not bloom in this manner. Indeed, there are a large number of bamboo species which botanists have never seen in bloom at all. Other bamboos bloom almost annually, but produce hardly any seeds. As it happens, the production of seeds is an energy-consuming process for the plant, and so if a plant can avoid it, it does so – as is the case for many of the hardy bamboos which live through the winter. During the great blossoming of *Pseudosasa japonica* in Europe around 1985, all the plants bloomed, without forming seeds. Afterwards they appeared to die off entirely, but ultimately all the plants grew back again from their root systems. That is also the great difference from tropical bamboos: through their evolution, hardy bamboos have further adapted to moderate climate conditions, usually with abundant rainfall. By contrast, the tropical bamboos of India, which have to cope with very dry and wet seasons, display growth rhythms and flowering cycles which are more consistent with their climatological circumstances.

Seeds are therefore no option for the propagation of ornamental bamboos. There simply are hardly any seeds available. Moreover, offspring by seeds often differ greatly from the original mother plant. This can be seen very clearly among the progeny of *Fargesia murieliae*, which are practically all smaller or grow less well than the original plants. Propagation by seed is only used for several tropical bamboos, chiefly in India. Nevertheless, the importance of the generative phase should not be underestimated, for although florescence is to a great extent uncontrollable in bamboos, among plants flowering is the only manner to obtain hybrids and new varieties. Possibly there are various factors that cause or stimulate blooming, such as hereditary tendencies, or dry climatic conditions. There is ongoing scientific investigation into this question, but among bamboos the key that leads to flowering has not yet been found. It will only be when this key is found that we can obtain still more beautiful and better bamboos by hybridisation.

Fargesia nitida in bloom

Division and separation

Among species that are capable of overwintering, the most familiar and most obvious method of propagating ornamental bamboos is the division of the plant. In this, the plant is cut or separated in two. It should be obvious that this is not always an easy method. For tropical bamboos, with stems 30 m high and 30 cm in diameter, it is no simple matter to divide or separate the plants. Once research was even done into the use of dynamite to separate such giants. Fortunately in our region, such drastic measures are not necessary.

There are in general two forms of growth among bamboos, with clumping roots on the one hand and running

Labour-intensive propagation of bamboo by separation

Division or cutting can be done by using a spade or an axe. With these, the plant can be divided into several pieces. These pieces are then planted elsewhere, or set into pots. Ornamental bamboos in our region are somewhat less problematic than the giant bamboos of the tropics, where chainsaws and mechanical diggers are used, but also for the plants growing in our climatic zone machines can be of help. Dividing plants is a very labour-intensive process, for which a good deal of strength is necessary (and often the spade or axe will break), but a pneumatic log splitter, for splitting blocks of wood, is a very efficient tool for separating large bamboos.

For producing their bamboos, nurseries try to have uniform propagation material, with the mother plants for propagation smaller than the plants in nature. In this way, the splitting can be done more efficiently. For instance, plant material from species in the *Sasa* group can be efficiently propagated from small plants less than 20 cm tall. For the division of *Fargesia* plants, nurseries try to keep the height to 1 m or less. Among a number of tropical bamboos such as the South American *Guadua*, one can saw off the giant plants at ground level, so that the rhizome will create numerous new shoots, which can then be divided. But even then a good set of hedge clippers and considerable strength are indispensable attributes.

roots on the other. The first group have pachymorphic rhizomes or rootstocks. These are very short, less than 10 cm long, and the end node grows up onto a new stem. This means that the stalks grow very close together, and the plant forms a clump, analogous to a sod of grass. This is the type of rhizome (rootstock) and manner of growth that we find with the *Fargesia* group and in all tropical bamboos. This also means that these bamboos do not spread rapidly, although after dozens of years a clump of these bamboos can indeed take over a considerable area. The second group have leptomorphic rhizomes or rootstocks that continue to grow and branch underground. They thus form a real network of underground rootstocks, and side nodes on these rootstocks grow up into net stems. As a result these stems grow farther apart. By looking at the stems above ground, one can often trace the path that the rhizomes are taking, by following the spread of the stalks. With *Semiarundinaria fastuosa*, dozens of new stalks can stand in one beautiful, straight line up to 5 m long.

Dividing a pachymorphic plant is like pulling a piece of turf apart. Each piece of sod can form the beginning of a new plant, with new stalks, rhizomes and roots. With leptomorphic rhizomes the cutting or division is a somewhat more exacting operation, because the rhizomes or rootstocks often have grown very far apart from one another, and in separation it is not always clear how large the divided pieces should be.

For ornamental bamboos the division of plants is the most used technique, and the one applicable for most bamboos. In this sense, it is a universal method. But here too there are several important drawbacks. Division is not easy for the tropical giants. Moreover, for large-scale production, one needs a huge number of mother plants. After all, one can divide a plant only once a year. Finally, the introduction of new varieties is the work of several years.

Propagation by cuttings

A number of tropical bamboos can also be propagated from cuttings. In this process one takes pieces of the stem with one or more axillary nodes, which are then stuck partially into soil. Both stems and roots then develop from the axillary nodes. With some species pieces of stem several metres in length are buried horizontally. These are much-used methods in tropical regions, but they are often highly inefficient. Not all of the pieces of stem form new plants. Moreover, the new plants show little uniformity. The efficiency of this method is too low for large-scale propagation. Therefore, for several tropical species such as *Dendrocalamus asper*, a more efficient method has been worked out: here a hole is made into a piece of stalk

Fargesia robusta in a private garden in Putte, Belgium. Note the geometric pattern created by the stem sheaths. Height, 3 to 5 m

knotted at both ends; the stalk is then filled with water or a solution with natural substances that promote rooting. Propagation by stem cuttings is however not possible with hardy ornamental bamboos. In the case of tropical bamboos the axillary nodes often have a capacity to develop roots, and it is these roots that grow into a full-fledged root system in cuttings. But the hardy bamboos do not have this capacity – at least not in their above-ground stems. However, they do have nodes and rudimentary roots on the rhizomes. Since these rootstocks are actually underground stems and branches, taking rhizome cuttings is a highly suitable method for bamboos with creeping or leptomorphic rhizomes, such as bamboos of the *Sasa* and *Phyllostachys* groups.

Particularly for the propagation of *Pleioblastus* and lower *Sasa* species this can be an efficient form of large-scale plant production. Pieces of the rootstock are buried in pots containing soil substratum. New plants then develop on these rhizomes. Slight warming of the substratum in the winter period increases the success rate with this method. In principle, using rhizome cuttings is also possible with *Phyllostachys*, but this is not very efficient.

Rootstocks are storage organs for starch and energy for the plant. This starch is the product of photosynthesis, in which the plant takes in carbon dioxide from the air and transforms it into sugars and starch. As the latter is stored particularly in the rootstock, rhizomes which are cut from the mother plant can for a time release sufficient energy to form new plants from themselves. In nature, the growth of the bamboo stops in the autumn, and several nodes are already prepared to grow into new stalks the following spring.

Often a rhizome cutting is made so that it includes several side branches, for these side branches and leaves can continually provide for new energy. This way rhizome cuttings work still better. But ultimately the line between cuttings and separation begins to blur, because one is then really dividing or separating, which in itself is a more efficient method.

Micropropagation through tissue culture

The use of ever smaller pieces of plants led to ever improved techniques for the propagation of bamboo. The era when explosives were used to separate large plants was definitely past. But still, for large-scale propagation of bamboo for commercial mass marketing, the classic propagation techniques clearly had a number of disadvantages. They were very specific techniques, which had to be optimised for almost every species of plant, and for the rarest plants they offered no possibilities for rapid propagation and introduction to the market from a single selected specimen. The ornamental plant sector, however, driven as it is by new stock and new varieties of plants, relies precisely on rapid propagation techniques.

Furthermore, in addition to the ability to grow large numbers and 'programme' the introduction of new items, the quality of the plants and their appearance is an important challenge. In the past, bamboos in the shop were often very expensive potted plants consisting of several stalks with few leaves. Today the bamboos that are offered on the market are much fuller and have more stalks. This striving for higher-quality plant material arose particularly in the house plant sector, where quality and rapid propagation are the only manner for firms to grow and remain competitive. Optimising propagation techniques thus focuses not only on programmable generation, but the plants must be green, vigorous, and very uniform.

Beginning in the 1980s a feverish world-wide search therefore began for improved methods for propagating bamboo. The objective of this search was to obtain still smaller plants for propagation, for in the classic division method there is clearly an upper limit. A single piece of node or rhizome cutting will not produce a fast-growing plant.

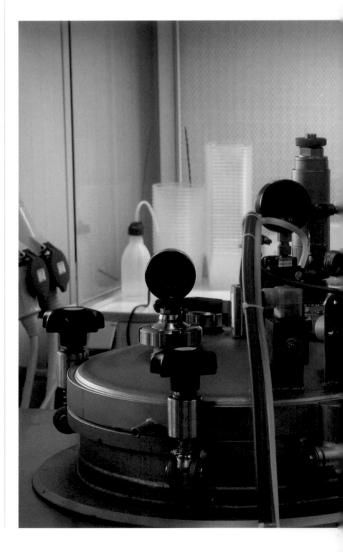

Sterile plastic dishes for the micropropagation of bamboo are filled by machine

Micropropagation by means of tissue culture, which had been responsible for a revolution in the cultivation of ornamental plants in the 1980s, appeared to be an obvious method to try. Today almost a billion plants world-wide are propagated by tissue culture, chiefly ornamental plants, but also bananas, oil palms and trees. A large percentage of the indoor plants that are on the market today come from tissue culture laboratories.

Tissue culture indeed succeeded in reducing the size of plants still further, to only several centimetres in height – thus the term micropropagation. In this method plants are grown in conditions that are free of micro-organisms such as bacteria and moulds. Under laboratory conditions the plants are propagated in glass bowls or jars (thus the term 'in vitro', which is Latin for 'in glass'). The chance that the house plants that you purchase on the market today were produced in this manner is very high. Familiar house-plants and cut flowers such as *ficus, Spathiphyllum, maranthas,* ferns, banana plants, *bromeliads, gerberas* and so many more are produced in tissue culture laboratories all around the world. In the Benelux alone there are already approximately twenty tissue culture firms, which each produce more than a million plants per year.

Ficus benjamina plants, for instance, are almost entirely propagated by tissue culture; in Europe that is a matter of about fifty million plants. Once produced in a tissue culture firm, the plants are then taken to other firms specialising in young plants, where they are 'hardened up' over a period of three to six weeks, thus becoming accustomed to ex vitro conditions. Both the roots and the photosynthesis (chlorophyll activity) of the plant are then developed fully. After that these young rooted plants are grown to commercially saleable plants, often by still other specialised businesses. *Bromeliads*, ferns and various woody plants such as rhododendrons and lilacs are also propagated in vitro.

The reason why micropropagation has become so completely established in the production of ornamental plants is that it is the best and most cost-efficient method by far for raising very uniform plants of high quality on a large scale. Consumers are continually becoming more demanding. Over the past decades there have constantly been more and better plants produced by means of tissue culture. Tissue culture was a real breakthrough for the ornamental plant sector in Western Europe.

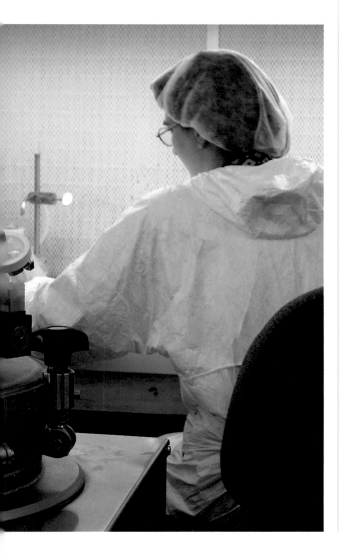

In Stage 1, bamboos are placed in test tubes

Tissue culture: some basic principles

Already at the beginning of the 20th century researchers had discovered that parts of plants, and even individual plant cells could grow and reproduce in a simple nutrient solution. This nutrient solution contained the necessary macro-elements (nitrogen, calcium, potassium, phosphorus), trace elements (such as iron and manganese) and sugars (as a source of carbon). In nature, these macro-elements occur in all soils, and they are the basic elements that every plant on earth needs in order to grow. Plants produce their energy, in nature, by transforming carbon dioxide from the air into sugars with the aid of sunlight. In tissue culture, the same sugars are added directly.

Plants grow not only with these elements, but they also make their own growth hormones or growth regulators. These permit them to begin growing in the spring, bloom and produce fruit, and halt their growth period in the autumn and prepare for winter. Plants regulate all this for themselves. In the 20th century scientific research into these growth regulators peculiar to plants caused a major revolution as we gained more insight into the growth and development of the plant. At the time, these were sensational discoveries, which today seem very ordinary to us. On the basis of this knowledge, growth regulators are now used on a large scale both in research and in the production of ornamental plants, trees and agricultural crops. Today these growth regulators can be made artificially. Thus, for instance, auxins are used in the rooting of slips from woody plants, and ethylene is employed for inducing blossoming in pineapples.

By adding these natural growth regulators, growth and development in tissue culture can be steered in a particular direction. If one wants only plants, but no roots, one adds chiefly what are called cytokinins. If one wants the plant with roots, one adds auxins, growth regulators which stimulate rooting.

In contrast to animals, with their very specialised kinds of tissue, plants are exceptionally inventive in nature too. Plants simply have more possibilities to propagate themselves than animals do, which are completely reliant on their sexual reproduction. For instance, begonias and African violets have long been propagated from leaf cuttings. If one sticks leaves in the ground, numerous new plants grow from them. Among certain sorts of *Kalanchoë*, the new little plants simply grow on the edge of the leaf.

Plants have still more of these unique, ingenious techniques for reproducing themselves. In principle, any cell of the plant can become a complete new plant, something

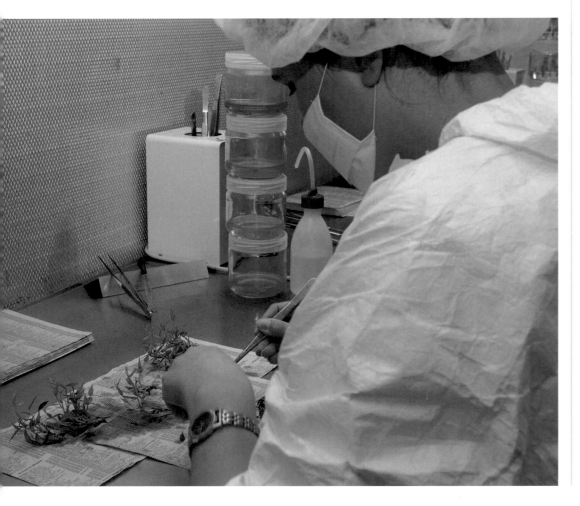

Under sterile conditions, once a month the bamboos are split and placed in new propagation medium

which is as of yet impossible with animals. In sexual reproduction, an embryo is formed by the joining of male and female gametes, in a process termed *embryogenesis* (literally, the creation of an embryo). In plants, embryos can also be created from body cells, in a process termed *somatic embryogenesis*. This is a process botanists are also familiar with from plants in nature.

In other cases, new plants can arise from groups of cells. This process, called *organogenesis* (the creation of new organs), is analogous with the leaf cuttings of African violets and begonias. In various bulbous and tuberous plants, one can produce complete new plants from flower stems.

Both somatic embryogenesis and organogenesis are possible ways of propagating plants in the laboratory. Most plants however are propagated by means of axillary budding, or side bud ramification. In this, the natural processes of the plant are copied perfectly, with smaller plants. New shoots grow from these plants through the development of side buds. If a hedge or fruit tree is pruned, multiple side branches grow out. Tissue culture resorts to the same process, but here it is guided. One gets, as it were, a complete nursery of miniature plants, each hardly a centimetre long, which are cultivated in glass trays.

Micropropagation of bamboo

Tissue culture opened up higly promising perspectives for bamboo. In place of the various techniques that were efficient for only particular species, tissue culture was to become a 'universal' method, not only for the cultivation of ornamental bamboo plants, but also for forestry and even for agriculture. For that reason, since the 1980s, hundreds of researchers and laboratories world-wide have been seeking this holy grail. In spite of their efforts, however, bamboo appeared to be a difficult plant, which does not permit itself to be miniaturised easily. Oprins Plant was one of the firms where intensive research was done, and in the mid-1990s the key was found. Today in principle all bamboos, both tropical and hardy, can be propagated in vitro.

The process of tissue culture begins with the collection of suitable material. One starts the process with selected mother material, the qualities of which are known. The plants selected are grown under optimal conditions in a glasshouse. We call this preparatory phase Stage 0. Pieces of stem and side branches with axillary buds are cut from these plants, sterilised and placed in a nutrient medium in test tubes. This is the first step (Stage 1). After several weeks or months the first side branches grow out to form a small tuft. This tuft can then be divided,

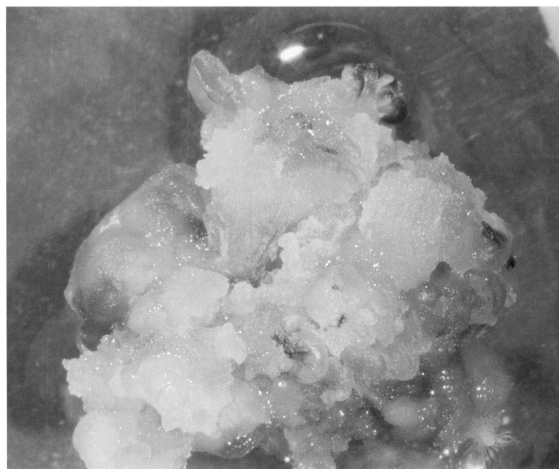

Somatic embryogenesis in bamboo

In barely a month the bamboos multiply three to five times

just as large plants can, albeit with a small knife or scalpel. Each step following Stage 1 takes place under sterile conditions, in which the instruments are disinfected and work is performed in a laminar flow cabinet. Inside it, the air is blown through a filter that screens out all bacteria and mould spores, so that the little plants can be propagated, and continue to grow, germ-free.

Once the plant is fully adapted to its in vitro surroundings, the multiplication phase follows (Stage 2). In this, the plant is divided and transplanted every month; typically, three to five new pieces are made from each piece, increasing the number of plants from one to five. If this process is continued for six months, by a multiplication factor of five you theoretically end up with 625 bowls each with ten plants. After seven months there are then 30,000 plants already. This is indeed a rapid multiplication process!

The plants are grown in climate-controlled rooms in which artificial lighting assures a daily rhythm of 16 hours of light and eight hours of darkness. In the nutrient medium, the plants are given all that they need. It is chiefly in this stage that cytokinins are used, natural plant growth regulators that stimulate branching. However, the plants have no roots. In the last phase in the lab (Stage 3), the plants are prepared for their transition to the glasshouse. This particularly involves slowing down the propagation process, and inducing the growth of roots on the plants. Auxins are used for the latter task, substances that are also used to encourage root formation in cuttings.

Stage 4 includes setting out the small plants in a glasshouse. The plants are set out in a turf substratum in trays, and they are kept under plastic for four to six weeks. This 'hardening' process permits the plants to regulate their own energy production and consumption. The rooting is crucial in this phase. In Stage 3 auxins were added in vitro in order to stimulate the growth of roots. These roots will mature fully during the hardening process. The plastic is gradually removed, permitting the respiration and photosynthesis to reach their proper level. After the hardening process, the plants receive further stimulants to continue growth, and after several months they are already 10 cm tall, and have become true young plants. To give an idea of this method's efficiency: on one table in the glasshouse there can be 5000 young bamboo plants. This same area could hold only several dozen pots for plants propagated in the classic manner.

Planting out the micropropagated bamboos for 'hardening'

High quality, low prices and new markets

After the hardening process, the plants are sent to nurseries, in southern Europe for *Phyllostachys*, or in western Europe for *Fargesia* and *Sasa*. The growing season lasts longer in southern Europe, and there is hardly ever a frost. Particularly *Phyllostachys* species grow better there. In the nurseries, the micropropagated plants are potted and grown until they become a marketable plant. The height and pot size for saleable plants depends on the market in which they will be sold. *Phyllostachys* plants between one and two years old are between 1.5 and 2 m tall, and find their way chiefly into wholesale distribution and supermarkets. The longer one lets a plant grow, the larger it becomes.

The plants are of outstanding quality, with many leaves, many branches, and in the middle of the pot. The leaves stay green longer than is the case with classically propagated plants, and growth is more rapid. This high quality, coupled with competitive prices, has made it possible to open up new markets. Where previously bamboo was a luxury plant, it is now widely available at reasonable prices. Sales and distribution take place on a large scale, through plant wholesalers and even auctions. The quality requirements that these markets set are especially high, but now bam-boo too can enter these sales and distribution channels for the first time, and it has become a plant that is affordable for everyone. While in the 1990s there was a careful run-up to larger numbers, it appears that in the coming years bamboo will become a true plant success, which thanks to these mass production methods can find its way into any garden. With this, we will have reached our goal. Without tissue culture that would have been impossible to realise. Just as in the cultivation of other ornamental plants, tissue culture has also changed the rules of the game with bamboo.

New Fargesias

After the mass flowering of *Fargesia murieliae* in the last decade of the 20th century, not only was a selection made from the new generation of seedlings, but plant collectors also went to search actively in the original habitat of the *Fargesia* in south-west China. It was in this region that the world-famous collector Ernest Wilson had found *Fargesia murieliae* in the early years of the 20th century. At the time he called it the 'most beautiful bamboo that I have ever seen', and named the species for his daughter Muriel. Collectors from Europe and the United States were then drawn to these inhospitable regions to find new varieties. These plants were spread among collectors, and tested for

Tens of thousands of small bamboo plants adapt to the greenhouse environment under plastic

ornamental value and their ability to survive winters. Up to the present, five interesting new varieties have stemmed from this process, which have meant a real enrichment of the range of ornamental bamboos available.

Two of these are *Fargesia* 'Rufa' and *Fargesia* 'Green Screen' (synonymous with 'Pingwu'), particularly elegant kinds of pachymorphic bamboos that are also exceptionally hardy. They can be used in hedges and for planting in beds, as solitary plants and as pot plants. These plants were separated by collectors, and within fifteen years several dozens were available. They were first propagated in vitro around 1998, and by 2000 there were already more than 50,000 plants available. Currently there are hundreds of thousands of plants from these two species produced every year at Oprins Plant. 'Rufa' and 'Green Screen' have already won various prizes at garden shows in past years.

Fargesias are the showpieces from BambooSelect™. Under this banner some forty quality species from the three groups of hardy bamboos are propagated on a large scale. Micropropagation plays a crucial role in this. The major advantages are rapid introduction to the market, particu-larly uniform plants, and an excellent price/quality ratio. This enables the large-scale introduction of the plants into new markets, so that ornamental bamboos are pos-sibilities for everyone's purse and for every garden. New species and varieties of bamboo can come on the market in only a few years time, a rapid introduction that was only a dream with the classic propagation techniques.

Bamboo for agriculture and forestry

Micropropagated bamboos are already an established fact in the ornamental plant sector in Europe. Every year large numbers of bamboos are produced, brought to saleable size and marketed in this manner. In addition to uniformity, quality and year-round production, micropropagation can also result in a considerable decrease in prices. Such price reduction is necessary for tropical silviculture, or for agricultural applications in temperate regions.

Bamboo is a special plant in tropical regions. More than a five-hundred million people derive their income from bamboo, and the vast majority of them are among the very poorest in the region. It is estimated that there are more

Successful hardening and rooting

Fast growing, quality bamboos can now be raised year-round

than a billion people who live in houses and huts in which bamboo is an important structural element. In such regions, bamboo is used in innumerable ways, from the manufacture of paper to the production of bio-energy. Further, bamboo has an important role to play in respect to ecology. With bamboo, the production of enormous quantities of biomass – bamboo is the fastest-growing plant in the world – is coupled with the absorption of large quantities of carbon dioxide. Massive planting of bamboo can thus be a measure against the greenhouse effect. Moreover, tropical bamboo uses water in a very efficient manner. In contrast to, for instance, eucalyptus, bamboo has a positive effect on the water balance in the soil.

For countries in the Third World, bamboo can also be an important plant in combating deforestation, and provide important leverage in the struggle against poverty. Various developing countries have therefore elaborated national programmes in cooperation with international organisations such as the World Food Organisation (WFO) and the Industrial Development Department of the United Nations (UNIDO). Through these programmes they are developing a sustainable and renewable raw material in their own country which can be used by the local population in many different ways.

The great bottleneck is undoubtedly the production of sufficient plant material for these programmes. In India, for instance, there are plans to plant six million hectares of bamboo in the coming seven years. About 500 plants are required per hectare, so that in total three billion plants are needed. This is absolutely impossible with the existing, classic propagation techniques. Not even a tenth of that number could be produced in that manner. As a result there is a great interest in the in vitro propagation of bamboo.

In the past decade numerous smaller, experimental bamboo forests were set up by Oprins Plant, each of them in collaboration with local partners. These plantations were set up in twenty countries all over the world, in Asia, Africa, Central and South America. Each time the great advantages of tissue culture became obvious: rapid propagation, easy transport and great vitality. Even in the volcanic rock of Bali, where for the rest nothing grows, bamboo thrives and aids in the greening of the earth.

But the story does not end with tropical forestry. Before the last Ice Age, bamboo was also a plant which was found naturally in Europe, as fossils prove. Once again today bamboo can play a role in Europe, not only as an ornamental plant, but also as a renewable source of biomass. In the 1990s, with the support of the European Union, a large-scale research project was established, 'Bamboo for Europe', with researchers from all over the continent. Test plantings were made in western and southern Europe. This research demonstrated that bamboo is a very suitable plant for European agriculture. Bamboos such as *Phyllostachys* can be a renewable and sustainable source of biomass. These plants grow to between six and ten metres in height, and harvesting them can be completely mechanised. The experiments that were done in the wood processing industry were all highly promising. Whatever wood is used for, bamboo is a strong and particularly environmentally-friendly alternative. Bamboo also appears highly suitable as a source of bio-energy, better than willow or poplar.

This research is being carried further in the existing plantations, and in new test projects around western Europe. In southern Europe bamboo is already being used in water purification installations for domestic waste water, and for the recycling of water in vineyards. The large-scale application of bamboo in European agriculture in the middle to long term also depends largely on the availability of plant material. Through classic propagation there is no way of providing enough bamboo for forestation or agriculture, the high cost renders it uneconomical. But here too micropropagation appears to be able to deliver the breakthrough: high-quality plant material at low prices for farmers.

Beyond propagation

There are a number of techniques available for the propagation of bamboo, but they are often applicable only for certain species, and are not suitable for large-scale propagation. Micropropagation through tissue culture has in recent years proven its soundness in the cultivation of ornamental plants, and will undoubtedly play an important role in large-scale reforestation projects world-wide. Oprins Plant has performed important pioneering work in the tissue culture of bamboo.

The results of research into the physiology and tissue culture of bamboo offer a range of other possibilities. For example, we are obtaining more and more insight into the blossoming and flower development in bamboos, so that not only growth processes but also the flowering process can be controlled. Just as with the propagation of bamboo, where fundamental research ultimately led to

successful micropropagation, groundbreaking research at Oprins Plant will in the long term make it possible to begin with the hybridisation of bamboos – not only cross-fertilisation among bamboos, but also hybrids between bamboos and grasses of other sorts, such as rice and sugarcane. In these, the best properties of bamboo can be conveyed to other important agricultural crops. One of the most important driving factors in human civilisation worldwide is agriculture, with its continual improvements and introduction of new plant varieties. Since the end of the 19th century, we have understood how cross-fertilisation and the process of inheriting characteristics takes place in plants. The development of maize from a plant hardly 1 m tall into the maize which is today grown in agriculture in temperate regions, and the fruit, vegetables, ornamental plants and trees that we currently plant in our gardens or grow in handsome pots are all the results of hybridisation and selection.

Giant bamboos play an important role in the old folktales of many peoples. They are the gifts of the gods to man. There are countless ways in which this fast-growing plant can be used as a renewable and sustainable resource, and it offers vast numbers of possibilities for bettering the world in which we live. Through further research, and ever improved applications, we can further perfect this gift, as a gift to our children and grandchildren.

Jan Oprins

Oprins Plant: Technology in the service of nature

The story of Oprins Plant began a quarter of a century ago when the business's present manager, Jan Oprins, started a small nursery along with his garden design firm. Initially the new nursery primarily provided plants he needed for his own work. But as a collector with a passion for plants in his blood, Oprins let a wide selection of plants filter through into the nursery. Thus from the very start bamboo was one of his favourite plants. Gradually the firm began to provide stock for other plant suppliers and garden centres, and the assortment available constantly expanded. The clients were drawn by the good quality and service they received for the price.

Today the firm is known around the world for its bamboo production. The present bamboo collection comprises something like 380 species, from hardy to tropical sorts. Of these, about 80 kinds are grown in large numbers. Although for outsiders it appears simple to propagate bamboo, it is not easy to grow bamboo of uniform quality in large numbers in a short period. The production of mother plants demands years of time. At the end of the 1980s, in collaboration with Professor Debergh of the University of Ghent, Oprins Plant began a research programme into a more efficient method of propagation,

namely in vitro propagation. The first successes came after more than eight years of research and much trial and error. In 1998 the firm in Rijkevorsel put an ultra-modern laboratory with a 'hardening' glasshouse into service. Today Oprins Plant is among the world leaders in the field of in vitro propagation of bamboo. This method has the advantage of producing new and better sorts of bamboo quickly, and in large numbers. In addition to growing ornamental bamboos, the technology developed is being used for bamboo as a reforestation plant. Sales are primarily to Asian countries, but Africa and South and Central America also take a portion of the stock.

Twenty-five years later, the situation has changed fundamentally. The firm has grown into a name to be reckoned with as a producer and supplier of garden plants. It has made strides toward providing a whole tree nursery assortment for other plant suppliers and garden centres. In addition to bamboo production, there are other specialities. *Ilex* or holly is a second product for the firm. Holly is ideal as a hedge plant. It makes a beautiful, thick wall that remains green year round. The firm's own hybridisation programme with various *Ilex crenata* species has already produced a first striking new plant. *Ilex crenata* 'Blondie'® is a seedling with soft yellow growing points, which give the plant a light sheen the whole summer. At the moment the firm has around 30 species in its range. With the production of oak leaf hydrangeas, the firm is providing another product which can also be propagated in vitro. This results in fine, well-branched plants. At the moment there are five varieties available. *Hydrangea quercifolia* is a plant on the rise in the Low Countries. It offers beautiful flowers (the flower buds are produced rather late in the spring, which almost eliminates the danger of frost damage), is well adapted to living through winter conditions, and has a magnificent autumn colouring. With regard to ornamental trees for streets and parks, the firm provides an ample assortment of more than 100 tall species.

The nursery in Belgium now covers more than 100 hectares and has just under 50 employees. Oprins Plant also currently has branches in several European countries. For example, the French branch, Rezo Plant, in Castillonnès, is an important bamboo production unit and base of operation for the French market. For several years there has been extensive bamboo production in north-west Spain. Activities have also begun on other continents, so that in 2004 we can rightly speak of Oprins Plant as an internationally renowned enterprise.

Water droplets clinging to the leaves of *Fargesia*

Bamboo and its environmental benefits

Bamboos are plants that can adapt to diverse environmental conditions, and they are a part of highly diverse ecosystems all over the world. By using bamboo in our landscape, we can often find answers to many of the challenges created by man. Bamboo can also provide ecological protection. Planting bamboos for aesthetic reasons, as attractive landscape plants, can pay an extra bonus if, by doing so, we can also safeguard, improve and upgrade ecosystems designed by man, provide soil cover, and purify the air.

Horticulture is the cultivation of plants for use in landscapes which we develop and realise ourselves. Worldwide, the use of bamboo in horticulture has great potential. Since the beginning of civilisation, people all over the globe have shaped the landscape around them and brought plants from the woods closer to their homes, both for their utility, and for their aesthetics. It is interesting to study this evolution, to discover how artificial landscapes bear within themselves the values of the cultures that planned and built them, and see what a landscape reveals about the evolution of society. The wide distribution of bamboos around the world, as well as the diversity of environmental conditions in which bamboos can grow, give this group of plants – the bamboos – unique advantages, and allow them to play a vital role in the future of our landscapes.

Bamboo offers what no other plant can. With bamboo we introduce a plant with unequalled potential in our landscape, including
– rapid growth
– vertical growth to screen or fence in, provide privacy and protect us against the wind

Li river, Xiping, China

- resistance against drought and pollution, since the plants are hardy and long-lived
- a root system with rhizomes (underground rootstocks) which combats erosion on slopes and open spots in the woods
- formation of groves, creating wooded sites which are most attractive to animals and various sorts of birds for nesting
- a capacity to recycle considerable carbon dioxide (12 ton/hectare), and thus purify the air, producing 35% more oxygen than trees in the same situation
- edible, tasty shoots, and thus a source of food
- a real renewable resource, which permits localised harvest for use for everyday requirements, as a plant for agriculture and forestry, and as a tool in biotechnology
- sensory input for healing, meditation, and sanctuary

- wonderful decorative properties, with stems in astonishing tints of green, gold, black and red, with colourful streaks and textures, and with enormous or, on the other hand, tiny and delicate leaves, of green, or streaked with gold, cream or white.

The famous garden and landscape architect Jens Jensen introduced garden and landscape architecture as environmental science, and investigated the concept of using landscapes designed by man to conserve and protect ecological systems. This is particularly of importance in urban and suburban landscapes, where streets and even motorways must be integrated into the planting. In such landscapes, bamboo can improve the environment in many ways. Because many species of bamboo have root systems with underground rootstocks that spread aggressively,

various sorts of bamboo are an ideal choice for massed planting, planting alongside, or in the central reservation of large roads, etc. The right selection of species can contribute to stabilising the soil and controlling erosion on highway berms, and further provide a barrier against traffic noise pollution. The right choice of bamboo species can also hide or eliminate unwanted prospects or views. Used as a hedge, bamboo can protect privacy, or mark out a certain route for foot traffic. As has been known for ages in Japan, bamboo can be used as a very effective ground cover requiring little maintenance.

Ground cover that requires little care

Dwarf bamboos, the low-growing species which spread by their rhizomes, are outstanding as ground cover, and offer an alternative that requires little maintenance in our landscapes. With the annual growth cycle of bamboos of this sort, there are new shoots no more than two times a year, and maximum height is reached in one season. Most hardy bamboos have the additional advantage of being evergreen. It is suggested that the growth from the previous year should be trimmed off each spring in order to show off the luxuriant new green leaves to their advantage. To add colour there are also very decorative forms (such as for instance *Pleioblastus viridistriatus*) with multi-hued or golden leaves.

These dwarf bamboos are very resistant to drought, and once they are well established need little water. Cutting bamboo ground cover short (or mowing it) allows one to control the height, and assures an attractive appearance. However, mowing is not required. Dwarf bamboos require extremely little maintenance, and are thus an outstanding alternative for more traditional ground covers. The very small *Pleioblastus distichus* is an unbeatable alternative for grass in public green spaces, on dikes and really on any surface where a large, green cover is needed.

Protection against soil erosion

The extensive underground rhizome and root system guarantees that bamboo is a good option for combating damage by water erosion in environments where rapid landslips and gully-forming occur. Bamboo is very effective at binding soil, and in that way holds the earth together on vulnerable riverbanks, deforested areas and on steep slopes. Bamboo can be an important element in biotechnology for soil management and stabilisation.

Windbreaks

Because of the considerable elasticity and strength of bamboo stalks, this plant can withstand very strong winds. The flexibility of the stalks helps them to bend without breaking even in a relatively strong wind, and without being uprooted as trees are. Bamboo can be planted as a windbreak, and because of its rapid growth it is an outstanding choice, often used to break the force of the wind along the boundaries of farms, and to protect cropland against wind erosion during periods when the ground is lying fallow.

(Above) Roundabout with *Pleioblastus pumilus* in Waddinxveen, The Netherlands
(Below) Business car park planted with *Sasa tsuboiana* (foreground) and *Phyllostachys aureosulcata* 'Aureocaulis'

Watersheds

Bamboo is often used on watersheds in order to improve the catchment of rain water, decrease the impact of heavy rain on the ground and soil erosion, and enhance their refilling with water. Some sorts of bamboo can tolerate constant flooding, which is important for the reinforcement of riverbanks, dams, dikes around lakes and ponds.

Swampy areas

Bamboo can be used to transform poor soil or wasteland into productive arable land. Because bamboo can grow in poor soil, it can be planted as an agricultural product, to be harvested for biomass. In this way a great deal of leaf litter and an extensive root system are created. Together these contribute to building up organic carbon in the soil and increasing the amount of microflora present, as well as improving the water management by the soil, such as increasing its water capacity and acidity.

Agricultural and forestry systems

Bamboo is an outstanding choice for sustainable agriculture and forestry. It can be harvested within three to five years, as opposed to the ten to twenty years for some softwoods. Thus it is an ideal resource for the wood and paper industry. Oprins Plant is presently researching the use of bamboo as a source of biomass for the wood industry, for instance in fibre and chipboard, and for biochemical products, or as a biological energy source for Europe (the Bamboo for Europe Project).

Biological treatment of waste water

An adult bamboo plantation can purify waste water while in the meantime producing a usable plant. Cobelgal, in Portugal, is actively investigating this important potential.

Covering rubbish dumps

Because bamboo grows quickly and has shallow roots, it can be planted as a green cap over rubbish dumps full of waste. It can easily grow without maintenance, and after being mechanically harvested is immediately usable as biomass for the wood industry, as an alternative and renewable source of fuel, for cattle fodder, and for other applications.

The enormously diverse potential of bamboo in horticulture is not yet being fully realised anywhere in the world today. This family of plants is exceptionally diverse in the number of varieties; from these we can select the ones that cater to the needs of a particular situation. Thus a place for bamboo can be found in almost every environment. The present status of the natural environment around the world is a universal concern, and bamboo is a plant with considerable environmental potential, which can help to create a better world.

A toupee of *Fargesia murieliae* in the zoo at Duisburg, Germany

Phyllostachys bissetii

Bamboo in our world

Bamboo does not have the same function in Europe as it does in Asia. While there it is a plant that is intrinsically interwoven with the life of every person, at an everyday level, the importance of bamboo in our region is more limited and unobtrusive. Although we have also learned to better understand and appreciate some aspects of this relative of the grasses – one can think of bamboo parquet floors; canned, edible bamboo shoots; bamboo paper and other applications – for us bamboo is first and foremost an ornamental garden plant. How we use bamboo in a garden – whether that is a private garden or a park, a plantation on an embankment or a single plant in a pot on a terrace – all depends on the nature of the plant. Does the bamboo spread, or not – in other words, how easily can it be controlled? There are further practical considerations that will play a role in choosing a bamboo. How high does it grow, how large are the leaves? Beyond that, the ornamental characteristics also play an important role in the choice. Does it perhaps have varicoloured leaves, or beautifully coloured stems, or grow in a particularly graceful form? One can find a number of types of bamboo that are suitable for every application. Thus it is time for a further introduction.

Fargesia

For most applications, and certainly for those in the smaller ornamental garden, the first varieties to be considered are those with a pachymorphic rhizome system. These are the non-spreading bamboos; in other words, plants that are rather easy to keep under control, possibly even without using a rhizome barrier.

In our climate it is primarily species from the genus *Fargesia* that will be of interest to us. They are among the most hardy sorts, and survived the cold winters in the early 1980s without any appreciable difficulties. They have more problems with periods of intense heat, but at least as of now that is not a real problem in our region. In general, they are also tolerant of drought. Depending on the sort, their height can vary from about 1.5 to as much as 8 m. In most types, the stem attains a diameter of up to 5 cm. They are a very elegant addition to a garden, often with a very graceful appearance, with many side branches and a mass of rather small leaves whose weight – particularly after a rain shower – makes the stems bend outwards.

There are various opinions – as we might expect – about the number of varieties, running from six to as many as eighty. A number of plants that lose all their leaves during hard winters are presently placed with the more primitive genus *Borinda*. Thus one can describe them as less hardy than the varieties within *Fargesia*. Another distinction with bamboos from the genus *Fargesia* is the presence of vertical ridges on the internodes of the stem or branches.

Fargesia murieliae 'Grüne Hecke' is a variety perfectly suited for an ever-green hedge up to 3 m.
Private garden, Rijkevorsel, Belgium

Fargesia angustissima is a very elegant variety, but not as well adapted to facing winters. In its homeland China (more specifically, in the ever-green deciduous forests of Sichuan) it can grow as much as 7 m tall, and is characterised by small, narrow leaves, up to 5 cm long and 0.5 cm wide. New stalks have a purple to greenish-purple colour, and while young are covered with a white waxy layer with vertical stripes. According to the recent classification, this plant would therefore belong rather to the genus *Borinda*.

In our climate the possibilities for using this variety are limited. Only in a very sheltered spot – for instance, an enclosed urban garden – can it be tried outdoors. The disadvantage here is then the height, which often does not fit with such a small space. This same disadvantage also militates against its use as a potted plant. In addition, this type is sensitive to drought. It is thus a variety that is for the true connoisseur of bamboo.

Fargesia denudata was introduced from the mountains of north-west Yunnan, China, in 1986 by the famous 'plant hunter' and 'plant man' Roy Lancaster. More introductions have followed since then. We could almost describe this variety as a stronger version of the more familiar *F. murieliae*. It is about 3 to 4 m high and displays exuberant growth, with small, medium green leaves. The stems become yellow when mature, particularly when the sun can reach them. A spot in full sun is not advised, but half-shade is just fine. I have observed that the plant can thrive in dry places, but does equally well in a damp spot, although it cannot stand having its feet wet all the time. It is absolutely proof against winters, and protects itself against cold and drought by rolling up its leaves, and dropping a part of its foliage in the winter, after the leaves turn a golden-yellow.

In general appearance then it looks very much like *F. murieliae*. The leaves are however broader and shorter. It also has more side branches and the leaves are grouped closer together. The impression that one gets from this plant is that it is also yellower than *F. murieliae*. *Fargesia denudata* is a good alternative for a more difficult place. It works perfectly as a solitary, but perhaps hangs over a bit too much for use as a hedge plant. It can certainly be used, however, for a wider, elegant screen.

The robustness of this species can perhaps be well illustrated by the following story. In February, 1990 – not immediately the most suitable period – during my student days in Grünberg, Germany, I received one stem of *Fargesia denudata* from Roy Lancaster, with a short root, which he brought along from his own garden. The plant was then new, and its characteristics not well known. This one stem has by now grown into a clump 1.5 m in diameter,

(Above) Its downward bending growth and long, narrow leaves make *Fargesia angustissima* very elegant. Height, 4 to as much as 7 m
(Below) *Fargesia denudata* is a good, drought-resistant species that was only named in 1986

from which a number of pieces have already been cut. It grows happily in a very sandy soil, which in the summer of 2003 could have been described more like dust than sand. It survived the dry, hot summer and the following dry spring without difficulty, and without supplementary watering.

Fargesia dracocephala is an undervalued variety. In nurseries it is often ignored in favour of others, such as *F. murieliae*. This is quite unjust. *Fargesia dracocephala* is a fine, hardy, high-growing bamboo with medium-green leaves. These leaves are about 10 cm long and 1.5 cm wide. They are arranged a bit like roof slates, thus forming a beautiful, closed leaf cover. The leaves do not roll up with drought or a sharp frost. When young the stems are covered with a heavy, blue-white waxy layer. In the sun these stems later can become red to black-red, but the plant is really more beautiful in half to full shade.

The way this plant grows is comparable with that of *Fargesia murieliae*, but it appears to grow somewhat more slowly. Unlike *murieliae*, the leaves do not curl up, and have a harder texture. It copes with winters well. *Dracocephala* is a beautiful, 'quiet' bamboo that can function well as a solitary, or for a wider screen. In its homeland, China, it is one of food sources for the giant panda. The types now being grown – 'Green Dragon', for example, is an excellent cultivated species by Oprins Plant – are seedlings, which came from the bloom in the 1980s. This means that a new blossoming is not to be expected – or should we say, feared.

Fargesia murieliae is the most popular garden bamboo. At least, that was the case until its flowering over the past years. The blooming began already in the 1970s and actually has continued on until this day. There is a new generation growing up – seedlings, in other words – which is very promising. But one must be careful: there are still plants from the older generation being offered, and these are unavoidably going to bloom.

Ernest Wilson, the man who introduced this bamboo into the United States, named it Muriel after the name of the daughter. He found it on April 17, 1907, in western Hubei, China, at an altitude of 2000 to 3000 m. He writes of it, 'It forms dense thickets on the mountains of north-western Hupeh, and with its clear golden slender stems is one of the most beautiful of Chinese bamboos'. Live specimens reached Europe in 1913, when the real success story began.

Fargesia murieliae is a very elegant bamboo, growing a maximum of about 4 m tall. The stalks are green, later fading to a yellow-green. They bear masses of small, soft pea-green leaves, the weight of which bends them outward.

(Above) *Fargesia dracocephala* 'Green Dragon' in a private garden, Weelde, Belgium. Height, 2 to 3 m
(Below) *Fargesia murieliae* was named for the daughter of E.H. Wilson, a plant-hunter in China at the beginning of the 20th century. Private garden, Meer, Belgium

Under the weight of the foliage this bamboo takes on the shape of a parasol, leading to its English nickname, the 'umbrella bamboo'. It should be given a prominent place in your garden, but not in full sun. It prefers half-shade, for in the sun the leaves quickly roll up. That also happens under other less favourable conditions; for instance the plant protects itself against the worst cold by dropping leaves, after they first turn a golden yellow. In general, however, *Fargesia murieliae* is perfectly able to survive our winters. It should also be given space, because after a few years the clump can reach a diameter of several metres. If it takes too much room, of course one can always cut pieces off, with-out in any way affecting its ornamental value or shape.

Irrespective of the perils of flowering, *Fargesia murieliae* is and remains a beautiful bamboo, particularly as a solitary. Various named varieties are available on the market, not all of which are equally valuable. Some of them belong to the older generation, and thus can begin blooming. Caution is advised. 'Grüne Hecke' is an Oprins selection which belongs to the new generation and does not produce runners. This means it is wonderfully suited for making a screen.

Incidentally, this type is a good illustration of the perils surrounding the names in bamboo. Among the names which are used for it are *Arundinaria murieliae*, *Sinarundinaria murieliae*, *Thamnocalamus spathaceus*, *Fargesia spathacea*, *Arundinaria sparsiflora* – and this list probably not even complete.

Fargesia nitida is a much-loved garden bamboo, with fine, dark green leaves and dark red-purple or red-brown stems. When they are young, the stems are at times covered with a blue-white, waxy layer. It has been known in Europe since the end of the 18th century. In nature, the plant is found in China, in forests at an altitude of 2400 to 3400 m.

It grows upright, without bending over as many other *Fargesia* do. According to the literature, it can grow to 4 m, but usually in our climate it reaches only about 3 m. In the first season of growth the young stem forms no side branches, something which we see with other species of *Fargesia* as well. The young stems standing bolt upright in a clump of older, leafing stems only strengthens the general impression of sprays of water in a fountain. In its homeland, China, *F. nitida* is another of the food sources for the giant panda. But this is a problem, because at the moment this sort is involved in a mass flowering. The blooming of a pachymorphic bamboo leads to the dying back of the plant, or at least its above-ground sections. Our pandas are thus facing a difficult food situation in regions where this species predominates.

(Above) *Fargesia nitida* 'Great Wall' as hedge. Private garden, Rijkevorsel. Height, 2 to 3 m
(Below) *Fargesia nitida* as the backdrop for a clump of *Miscanthus sinensis*, Kalmthout Arboretum, Belgium

Fargesia robusta 'Pingwu' (behind, left) with *Pennisetum alopecuroides* (foreground) and *Phyllostachys aureosulcata*
'Spectabilis' (behind, right). Private garden, Veerle Laakdal, Belgium

But the blooming is also a problem for our gardens. It appears that the flowering period for *Fargesia nitida* could well continue for a number of years. Planting it in its traditional form really cannot be advised. Fortunately, there are already specimens of the new generation coming on the market. With them we can rule out flowering in the years to come.

Fargesia nitida 'Great Wall' (in the Oprins selection) is a beautiful specimen from the new generation. It has the typical upright growth and does not proliferate wildly. Oprins selected this plant several years ago on the Isle of Man, and immediately saw its potential as a hedge or screen: thence the name. The stems and leaves are dark green. 'Great Wall' is a plant which can also fit into a garden as a solitary. It is best planted in a spot in the semi-shade and provided with a damp ground rich in humus, just as one would plant any of the types whose leaves curl up with drought or frost. These conditions are to be remembered if one wants to set out 'Great Wall' as a potted plant on a terrace.

There are quite a few other named varieties of *Fargesia nitida*, such as 'Anceps', 'De Belder', 'Chennevières', 'Eisenach', 'Ems River', 'McClure' and 'Nymphenburg'. Because it is more than likely that these belong to the same generation as the types now blooming, caution is advised.

Fargesia robusta 'Green Screen' *('Pingwu')* is a selection from Oprins Plant from this Chinese species. It is one of the larger bamboos within the genus, with a height of 3 to 5 (and even 6) m, and a stem thickness of up to 2.5 cm. Once again, it is a source of food for the giant panda. In contrast to, for instance, *F.* 'Rufa', this type grows upright. The leaves are a glossy bright green and can be 8 to 20 cm long and 6 to 20 mm wide. The cultivated variety 'Green Screen' is set apart by its stem sheaths. These are white and show up well against the background of the young green stalks. Their pattern along the stem is very regular, geometric. This makes the visual impression given by the young stalk very spectacular. An additional charac-teristic is that the plant begins to form new shoots very early in the season. That could be problematic in periods with late overnight frosts and in open situations, but in recent years there have been no problems of this sort reported. In winters that are not too extreme, the plant is perfectly hardy. It should be given a sufficiently roomy location, in a sunny to lightly shaded spot. As its name indicates, 'Green Screen' can be used as a fence or broad hedge, but it also looks very good as a solitary. This plant is really a must for the garden of every bamboo lover, if only for the striking pattern of the young stems with their decorative contrast between the white stem sheaths and the green of the stalk itself. It is not to be

(Above) *Fargesia robusta* in combination with other bamboos
(Below) *Fargesia* 'Rufa' with *Hyarangea serrata*. Private garden, Zandhoven, Belgium
p. 70-71: *Fargesia murieliae* as border planting around a pond. Wirtz project, private garden, Meer, Belgium

confused with any other *Fargesia*. The species itself, *Fargesia robusta* (Campbell) can also be recommended.

From a botanical perspective, the place of *Fargesia* 'Rufa' is not entirely clear; we are still not certain about the taxonomic position of this plant. We are speaking here of the form that is raised in our part of the world as an ornamental plant. Is it a species or not? Some authors regard it as a hybrid of *F. rufa* and *F. dracocephala*. Thus here we are using the term 'Rufa' as the name of a cultivated variety, while other authors consider it as a peripheral form of the species and will give the name as *Fargesia rufa Yi*, in which 'Yi' is the name of the writer who first described this *Fargesia* as a species, Yi Tongpei. This bamboo was recently (1995) introduced to the West from the Chinese province of Gansu. It grows there at an altitude of 1000 to 2200 m, in forests or among bushes. It is a food source for the giant panda. The plant is also found in Sichuan.

In the garden it proves itself to be a decorative bamboo, very capable of withstanding cold weather, with great vitality. Even in hard winters it retains its beautiful appearance, since the elegant light green leaves do not change colour or fall off. Another notable quality is that, in contrast to other species such as *F. murieliae* or *F. nitida*, the leaves do not curl up under difficult conditions. *Fargesia* 'Rufa' is certainly an asset for a garden. It grows about 2 to 3 m high, and demands a lightly shaded place. With its graceful, bending shape, it looks very beautiful next to a pond. It is also suitable for use as a potted plant for a terrace, but there one must see to it that it has sufficient water. Other possible ways to employ it are as a screen or hedge, or just as a solitary in the midst of other, lower planting. The stem sheaths provide an additional decorative value. They are first red-brown, and evolve to a straw colour. They remain on the young stem for an unusually long time.

Fargesia (scabrida) 'Asian Wonder' is a Chinese species from the mountains of Sichuan and Gansu, among other places. It grows to form clumps, and has decorative, narrow leaves of a beautiful blue-green hue. They are up to 18 cm long, by a maximum width of something less than 2 cm. Its height comes to about 3 m. The young shoots are purple coloured. The green stems have a grey-blue waxy layer on the lower part of the internodes, which contrasts beautifully with the red-brown colour of the branch sheaths. This hardy plant thrives best in complete shade or half-shade and can be used as a solitary or for a screen. It is an elegant acquisition in the selection, standing out particularly for the splendid colour arrangements of sprouts, stem and branch sheaths.

(Above) *Fargesia scabrida* 'Asian Wonder' has splendid stem sheaths. Height, 3 to 4 m
Private garden, Valkenswaard, The Netherlands
(Below) *Fargesia* 'Jiu' with ground planting of *Asarum europaeum*.
Private garden, Valkenswaard, The Netherlands

In the second half of the 1980s several exciting new sorts of bamboo were introduced as seedlings. *Fargesia* 'Jiu' (synonymous with *F.* 'Jiuzhaigou') is the present trade name for a gorgeous bamboo which comes from Jiuzhaigou Natural Park in the northern border area of the province of Sichuan, China. At first sight this bamboo looks like a form of *F. nitida*, but there appear to be enough elements that can be identified to distinguish it. first, the stems of *Fargesia* 'Jiu' make it stand out: the young stalks are first green, in the spring they change colour to an orange-brown, and later to red. This is particularly clear when this plant is given a somewhat sunnier place in the garden, a condition with which it can cope very well, in contrast to other sorts of *Fargesia*. If one is looking for an elegant bamboo as a solitary, not too tall (2 to 3 m), for a place in the sun, this is the perfect choice. The leaves are small and the shape very dense and erect. At present, this is a very good alternative for *Fargesia nitida*, because up to now there has been no indication that 'Jiu' is going to start blooming in the near future. To date, it has proven itself capable of withstanding winters, even in exposed places in the north. In addition to being used as a solitary, because of its erect growth 'Jiu' can also be considered for use as a hedge plant. Its non-spreading character is an additional advantage in this usage.

Important notice: from this same natural park there were many other seedlings introduced, and they are not all as beautiful. It is therefore important to choose the right type, namely Type 1.

Indocalamus

At first sight plants from the genus *Indocalamus* display some similarity with those from the genus *Sasa*. Both genera are in part characterised by broad leaves and a single main stem per bud, except at the top of the stalk where there may be up to three branches per bud. With *Indocalamus* the length of the leaf blade is more than four times its width. (With *Sasa* it is usually less than four times.) Because its leaves suffer less from dying off at the edges and tips than those of *Sasa*, *Indocalamus* gives a fresher, healthier impression.

Indocalamus latifolius is less prone to running as it grows than most species within this leptomorphic genus. Instead, it tends to form beautiful clumps. It is a typical shadow plant, coming from central and eastern China. With a maximum height of 3 m, it can be termed a mid-height variety. The very large, deep green leaves can be as much as 30 cm long and about 5 cm wide. Because of their size they hang somewhat. In late autumn and winter, its frost-covered leaves are therefore very beautiful. In China the stems are used to make chopsticks, brushes and pens. The leaves are used in making mats, hats and as packaging for food. It is an attractive variety as a solitary, but also well suited for planting in beds and even as a taller ground cover.

Fargesia murieliae as ground planting for an existing stand of trees. Wirtz project, private garden, Meer, Belgium

Fargesia murieliae 'Bimbo' with ornamental grasses and *Phyllostachys nigra* (behind)

Jos van der Palen's Collection Garden

'We want a very tall bamboo. That's what people often ask when they come in here,' says Jos van der Palen, owner of the Kimmei bamboo nursery in Valkenswaard. 'If you inquire a bit more, it turns out that they are looking for a bamboo about 2 m tall. And then you quickly settle on *Fargesia*.'
The next question that clients ask us is where to put the bamboo. Should it be in the sun or in the shade? 'The best place for a *Fargesia* is half-shade to shadow. But there are also species that can tolerate the sun. But for them you have to have soil rich in humus, and never let it dry out entirely,' van der Palen advises. *F. robusta* (Campbell), *F. 'Jiuzhaigou 1'*, *F. dracocephala* and *F. denudata* are reasonably sun-resistant. 'There is little demand for *Fargesia*

dracocephala,' van der Palen notes. 'People find it – quite unjustly, I think – too "ordinary". My own favourites are *F. robusta*, and particularly the Campbell variety, and *F. 'Jiuzhaigou 1'*. The only drawback of *F. robusta* (Campbell) is that it sprouts rather early, and thus sometimes has problems from late night frosts.
Fargesia rufa also takes the sun well. What does van der Palen really think about the botanical classification of this plant? 'Our plant is from a sort of intermediate area between the distribution ranges of *F. rufa* and *F. dracocephala*. I see it as a broad peripheral form of *F. rufa*. As a matter of fact, within the group of *Fargesias* we can indeed make several rough distinctions, but there are a lot of transitional forms and hybrids,' he explains. Classifying bamboos is no simple matter. For instance, *F. 'Jiuzhaigou 1'* was at first regarded as a form of *F. nitida*, but really it is a seedling that does not fit into a spectrum of that species. In view of the fact that *F. nitida* is presently flowering, for us that is a good thing. But still, in the future a broader definition of the species is needed. A major and clear distinction between the genera is whether the leaves roll up or not under unfavourable conditions such as frost or drought. *Fargesia murieliae* tends to roll its leaves rather quickly, while, for instance, *Fargesia rufa* does not do so. Are the 'rollers' better resistant to frost or drought? The fact is that most people find the rolling up of the leaves ugly. Thus, *Fargesia murieliae* should not be planted in full sun.
According to Jos van der Palen the most important uses of *Fargesia* are found in their role as solitaries and as screens. He does not advise planting them in pots, except when extraordinary circumstances make it necessary or possible, for instance when one has only a terrace or balcony. The best sorts for potting then are *F. rufa* and possibly also *F. robusta* (Campbell).
'A real rhizome barrier in the classic sense is generally not necessary. In principle, a margin of about 10 to 15 cm is enough,' says Van der Palen. One could for example use a tile turned on its side. Each plant needs a minimum of 1 m², and must be rejuvenated about every four or five years. What that means is getting the old sections out, and that is not easy. Perhaps one can better just let it grow, and every now and then cut a piece off. With regard to spreading, there is really no absolute limit. There is also no relation between the height of the stem and the expansion of the plant.
'There are still more sorts of *Fargesia* coming in,' says Jos van der Palen. Then he shows us his newest acquisition, *Fargesia demissa*, which will perhaps prove to be the most hardy species for facing winters ...

Phyllostachys

For many garden and plant lovers, a 'real bamboo' must have stems that are several centimetres thick. For those who prefer bamboos with stems of sizable diameter *Phyllostachys*, rather than the varieties from the genus *Fargesia*, is the right choice. Furthermore, the stems of *Phyllostachys* are often splendidly coloured. No wonder then that this is among the favourites of bamboo lovers, and that they are planted frequently, both as solitaries and as screens.

The genus *Phyllostachys* is a very large one, with about 75 species and more than 200 varieties. They are distributed over a large area, in temperate and subtropical regions of eastern Asia, from sea level to an altitude of about 3700 m. It is an impressive sight in a garden, with a height of several metres and, depending on the species, up to more than 20 m, although the climate and the soil must be favourable to attain that. In gardens in the Benelux heights of up to 10 m are possible; in the south of France – for instance in the Bambouseraie de Prafrance, near Nîmes, 20 m is no exception. They are leptomorphic (that is to say, with spreading rhizomes) so that they can take over considerable areas. Fortunately, the rhizomes spread close to the surface, and thus it is fairly easy to keep the plants under control with a suitable rhizome barrier. However, this should be anticipated at the time of planting, because installing the barrier later generally means more problems.

Despite the wealth of forms, *Phyllostachys* as a genus is one of the bamboos that is easiest to identify, in particular because the stems have striking grooves between the nodes. These sulci (singular sulcus) are clearly present on one side of the stem and, remarkably, alternate 180° from one successive node to the next. Side branches appear at the node, on the side with the stem groove. They always come in pairs, sometimes with a smaller side branch that often drops off the stem as it gets older. The leaves can be said to be rather small in relation to the height of the plant. They are regularly replaced, but the replacement happens unobtrusively and year round, with a high point in the spring. The leaves are long and narrow, and have a net-patterned vein structure.

Phyllostachys aurea breaks up the harsh lines of the dwelling. Private garden, Beerse, Belgium. Height, 4 to 6 m

Phyllostachys aurea is aptly named the Golden Bamboo. This may seem strange, as neither the leaf nor the young stalks have a golden colour. On the contrary, they are green. Only the older stems – and then, only when they are exposed to the sun – can become a golden yellow. The lower part of the stems is very characteristic for this species. Here the internodes (the sections between the nodes) are shortened and thicker than usual, and this explains the use of the stems in Asia, where they are favoured for the handles of parasols and walking sticks. In the garden one can remove the branches in this shortened section for aesthetic reasons, if desired. The leaves are long and narrow, and green. The species is Chinese in origin, from the provinces to the south of the Yellow River. It was introduced into Europe already before 1870.

This variety is resistant to heat, cold and drought, and in our region grows to about 4 to 6 m in height, although in other climatic conditions a height of 8 m is possible. An additional advantage is that in Northern Europe it hardly spreads, in contrast to its behaviour in warmer climes. It can be used nicely as a solitary or a screen, if only because it has an erect growth pattern. It perhaps functions better as a screen than other varieties of *Phyllostachys* because, with the shorter internodes on the lower part of the stem and the side branches which grow from them, it achieves a greater density.

As a solitary, *Phyllostachys aureosulcata* has greater ornamental value than the above. As the name itself indicates, the plant has a yellow sulcus which contrasts nicely with the otherwise dark green stem. Another identifying point is the zigzag structure of the lower part of some stems. The ornamental values depend more on the individual – it is in the eye of the beholder, if you will – because some garden lovers experience this zigzag structure as intrusive instead. It grows somewhat higher than *P. aurea*, about 5 to 7 m, and has a greater tendency to run wild. When used as a solitary, a rhizome barrier is certainly necessary. On the other hand, this manner of growing has advantages when it is used as a high screen. It is again a Chinese plant, coming from the region of Beijing and the province of Zhejiang, along the shore of the East Sea. The plant arrived in Europe at the beginning of the 20th century (although other sources give the date of introduction as 1866).

This is a typical example of a plant that is described as a species while it is really a variety. The original type, with completely green stems, was only known later. For lack of a better solution, it was named *P. aureosulcata* 'Alata' (and sometimes *f. alata*). It is claimed that under the right kind of circumstances this variety grows larger than the 'species'. Given the completely green character of the stems,

Phyllostachys aureosulcata 'Harbin Inversa' has stems with thin green vertical lines. Height, 5 to 7 m
p. 78-79: This ground planting of *Phyllostachys nigra* is regularly trimmed to keep it at this height. Fotomuseum, Antwerp

this is entirely logical. The applications are comparable, thus as a solitary or as a higher screen.

P. aureosulcata 'Aureocaulis' is a variety with completely yellow stems. However, this must be nuanced a bit, because it happens that green striping occurs on the lowest internodes. In our region, where the nights in the spring can be a good bit colder than the days, the young stems are sometimes coloured rose-red or purple-red. This also happens with other bamboos with yellow stems, and apparently has to do with temperature. This can also be seen as an additional advantage. The applications of this bamboo are comparable with the type.

P. aureocaulis 'Spectabilis' is more or less the opposite of the type. Here the stems are yellow and the sulcus is green. It is a very attractive and therefore much-loved garden bamboo, despite its propensity to get out of hand. Other varieties are 'Harbin' (green stems with yellow stripes, grooved) and 'Harbin Inversa' (yellow stems with fine green stripes in small grooves). Whatever its form, *Phyllostachys aureosulcata* is a beautiful bamboo with stems that are 3 to 4 cm in diameter, well capable of withstanding winter weather, and finely coloured. The colour patterns of *P. bambusoides* are perhaps even more outspoken, but this variety is less hardy, and requires warmer summers to grow well.

Phyllostachys bissetii is a trouble-free, very hardy high bamboo with a completely green appearance. It comes from China, more specifically from Sichuan and Zhejiang, but was named for David Bisset, manager of the introduction station in Savannah, Georgia, in the US, where it was introduced in 1941.

This is a high species, easily reaching 8 m in our climate, with dark green stems and leaves. It forms side branches already at its very lowest nodes, and therefore becomes very dense and massive in the course of only a few years. It grows very vigorously, and certainly requires a rhizome barrier. Because of its outstanding ability to survive winters, it can be used as a fence on the north side of a garden. It can also be planted as a solitary, although it has no eye-catching colour pattern. But in a soberer garden, in a difficult place, it has the added value of its imposing presence, and is by nature a plant which requires no special care. We can recommend it, even if only for the magisterial calm this species radiates.

In the genus, *Phyllostachys decora* is one of the species which expands fastest. A rhizome barrier is thus a necessity. But on the other hand, it is also one of the most drought-resistant species, an advantage that is not to be underestimated. This bamboo, introduced from China in 1938,

(Above) Leaf contrasts with *Phyllostachys aureosulcata* 'Spectabilis' and *Gunnera manicata*
(Below) The two-year-old stems of *Phyllostachys nigra* are strikingly black in colour.
Height, 4 to 6 m; stem thickness, 3 to 4 cm

has an erect growth pattern, and reaches a height of 8 m. Its Chinese name, meizhu, both means 'beautiful bamboo' and indicates that it is highly esteemed. That is primarily for its attractive stem sheaths. They are quite striking, particularly on young shoots: dark purple to pale green or white, striped with purples and green accents. The most beautiful stem sheaths are found on stems of a mature plant. It is decorative as a solitary, but its manner of growing also makes it usable as a screen. The masses of hanging leaves afford it a particularly elegant air.

Phyllostachys humilis is one of the smallest species in this genus, with a height ranging from 3 to 5 m, with stems that have a maximum thickness of a good 2 cm. The young stems are dark brown and later become green, sometimes orange-yellow in full sun. With its erect growth and relatively small size, this species can be particularly considered for use as a hedge or windbreak. It can be pruned or not, as desired. A word of caution: despite its relatively low stature, it spreads aggressively through its rhizomes, and a barrier is therefore certainly advised. It is thoroughly hardy, and the narrow green leaves stay beautiful the whole winter through. The origin of this plant is uncertain. It does come from China, but precisely what part is unclear. It is cultivated in Japan; there it is called Hime-Hachiku.

Phyllostachys nigra owes its name to the colour of its stems. At first they are dark green, but very quickly, in their second year, they turn to a deep, glossy black. In our climate an adult plant can grow to substantial size, but this depends on the circumstances in which it is grown, and the clone chosen. There appear to have been several types raised, and the height of 17 m that is sometimes reported in the literature therefore is generally far from being achieved. In its homeland, China, this species is increasingly rare, but it has been grown as an ornamental plant for a very long time, so that there is really no question of extinction. It does not spread too vigorously in our climate, but a rhizome barrier is still advisable. Its over-wintering qualities are good, although in somewhat harder winters leaf damage can occur.

There are a number of varieties and forms of this species. For instance, *P. nigra* var. *henonis* has stems that are not black, but which remain green. This plant is also a bit taller than the species. Even in our climate, 10 m is viable. Its growth pattern is more erect. One might question if this is not the real species, of which the form with stems which become black is a variety. But the rule of priority applies here: *P. nigra* was described as a species first, and only later did var. *henonis* come forward.

Phyllostachys iridescens is a robust bamboo with sometimes striking striped stems. Height, 6 to 8 m; stem thickness, 4 to 6 cm

Another beautiful type is 'Bory' (synonymous with 'Boryana'). This is also taller than the species, and reaches sizes that are comparable with those of var. *henonis*. The stems are clearly different. 'Bory' has green stems that are flecked with purple-black, in a pattern that is reminiscent of a leopard skin. Just as with the species, in a hard winter there can be some damage to the leaves. However, in the Kalmthout Arboretum in Belgium, during the winters of 1984-86 the stems themselves survived temperatures as low as −25 °C.

Phyllostachys vivax is a tall species with relatively wide, slightly pendant leaves, which gives it a somewhat tropical appearance. Because of the mass of leaves, young stems can sometimes suffer from rain and wind. If necessary, the top can be trimmed back to a certain extent. The plants grow quickly, and the name *vivax* refers to this rapid growth. The stem sheath is flecked in smoky tints. The internodes have obvious lengthwise grooves. This Chinese species comes from the provinces of Zhejiang, Jiangsu, Fujian, Henan and Shandong.
Especially the type 'Aureocaulis' must be counted among the most beautiful bamboos. Here the stems are entirely deep yellow, with the exception of fine green lengthwise stripes. If one takes into account that these stems are 5 cm in diameter, combined with large, pendant leaves, one will immediately understand the striking beauty of this plant. It does have the inclination to spread rapidly, so a rhizome barrier is certainly needed. It is quite hardy, and grows to a height of about 8 m.

(Above) *Phyllostachys humilis* is the lowest of its group, growing to between 3 and 5 m high
(Below) *Phyllostachys nigra* 'Henonis' is one of the most beautiful higher varieties with green stems.
Height 6 to 10 m; stem thickness, 4 to 6 cm
p.82-83: Cathedral effect of *Phyllostachys nigra* 'Boryana'. Kalmthout Arboretum, Belgium

p. 85: *Phyllostachys vivax* 'Huanwenzhu inversa'
is a new mutation from *Phyllostachys vivax* 'Aureacaulis'.
Height, 6 to 8 m; stem thickness 4 to 6 cm

Wolfgang Eberts

Wolfgang Eberts,
Phyllostachys and more

Baden-Baden may not be the cradle of bamboo in Europe, but the park near the castle of the Margrave of Baden is in fact the site of one of the oldest bamboo plantations. The variety involved is *Phyllostachys viridiglaucescens,* and the plantation has existed since 1904. Surprisingly, even at that early date there was something called the European Bamboo Society, which even published a newsletter with black and white photographs in Brussels. The bamboo plantation in Baden-Baden was described and pictured in an article in this magazine. Nevertheless, it is Eugène Mazel who in Europe is considered the pioneer for bamboo. By initiating the construction of Prafrance, a park near the southern French town of Anduze, Mazel began to spread bamboo in Europe already in 1855. At Lake Constance, the island of Mainau also had bamboo plantations in the early 20th century, and the head gardener there, Victor Nohl, must have been fascinated with these tree-sized grasses. He experimented particularly with their qualities for withstanding winter weather.

But then for a long time nothing more was heard of bamboo in Europe, and no one paid much attention to it. In the early 1960s *Fargesia* varieties appeared in publications, and slowly in gardens too. They were introduced via Denmark.

A person who played a very important role in this was Axel Olsen, director of the Royal Botanical Garden in Copenhagen. He received a plant from Vilmorin, France, and encouraged his friend Thyme, a plant breeder, to propagate it. Olsen was also interested in *Phyllostachys,* and planted many different varieties. That was in the early 1960s. The big breakthrough for *Phyllostachys* came in the 1990s when *Fargesia murieliae* began to bloom. This flowering and dying back lasted many years. Many private garden owners not only regretted the loss of their garden bamboos, but were at the same time amazed at what a complex phenomenon this mass flowering was. The media dwelt on this natural phenomenon. Prior to this, it was a rare case that a plant received so much attention from the public at large. The die-off of *Fargesia murieliae* was the chance *Phyllostachys* needed to step into the spotlight. Until then, there had really been only one bamboo for the average garden owner, *Fargesia.* Now it became clear that there had to be many more kinds. The German Bamboo Centre used the opportunity to promote the use of many other bamboos, and in particular *Phyllostachys.* For the various species that were already available the big concern was their survival in European winters. Many potential clients who lived in cold climates had a great interest in the tree-like grasses. One could say that they were a bit tired of conifers, yet fresh, spring greens in the middle of winter exercised a great attraction for them. Thus the hardy *Phyllostachys* began their career. Among them were *P. aureosulcata* 'Spectabilis', *P. aureosulcata* 'Aureocaulis', *P. humilis, P. bissetii,* and many others. The *P. aurea* that were grown in Italian nurseries and shipped northward were generally disappointing. They didn't always die in cold regions, but did show leaf damage and during the spring months looked poorly and untidy. After a while garden architects became interested in Phyllostachys, and today we thank them for the use of large numbers of this bamboo species.

When we speak of *Phyllostachys* in Europe, we generally also speak of rhizome barriers. No *Phyllostachys* at all should be planted without taking into account the extent of their underground growth. The rhizome barrier was first used in Kew Gardens, where sheets of 2 m were joined together. That is of course too labour-intensive. It was the German Bamboo Centre at the Eberts Baumschule in Baden-Baden that approached the plastics industry to produce high density polyethylene in rolls. After some experimentation it went into production. It is 2 mm thick and 70 cm wide, and is closed by means of two aluminium strips.

We have many climatic zones in Europe. In Ticino, in the lake region around Lugano, or in northern Italy, you can see *P. pubescens* of 15 to 20 m in height, with a diameter of 14 cm, almost as much as a stovepipe. Chinese visitors to Moso in Val Fontana Buona, near Genoa, have been amazed at what they saw, and had to admit that they grow better there than they do on Mogashan Mountain in the province of Zhejian.

Without doubt, bamboo, and particularly *Phyllostachys*, fits well with modern architecture. Our tall glass and steel structures need light green, and bamboo, combined with permanent plants and topiary, can provide a certain Asian touch.

Many years ago we planted *P. edulis* in our bamboo nurseries in Italy, in order to later harvest the plant's edible shoots. They are doing well, and the shoots are delicious, but not yet on the market. Once grown to maturity, the fresh green stems quickly find takers. Architects who have fallen in love with bamboo also want to use these indoors. This can be difficult, but certainly not impossible when attention is given to the nodes of the bamboo. Air indoors is very dry, and there is less light than the plant needs. With the

right adaptations, however, to provide increased ambient humidity, supplementary light, air circulation, planters of the right depth and so forth, bamboo can become a remarkable interior plant. The choice of suitable species is just as important as getting the environmental factors right. There are many kinds of bamboo, and knowing which is the right bamboo for the right place is of vital importance for success. What is most attractive about bamboo is the fresh green of the leaves and stalks. But at the same time, lots of people are charmed by their soft movements, or the sound when the stems rub against each other in the wind. Bamboo is no stranger any more. It is capturing ever more hearts, and more gardens. As is the case in planting any garden, it is important that bamboo be planted correctly: the choice of the right species, control of the spreading rhizomes, the right place, and the right care and maintenance. It is a plant with many qualities, and its owner will enjoy it for many years.

(Above) *Pleioblastus viridistriatus* becomes yellower as it receives more sun
(Below) *Pleioblastus variegatus* has a pronounced white-variegated appearance

Pleioblastus

The genus *Pleioblastus* is comprised of bamboos with lep-tomorphic rhizomes. They spread aggressively and absolutely need control. The majority are of Japanese origin. With plants of this genus it is not the stems that attract attention through their thickness or colour. The stalks are slender and are covered with leaves which are much larger in comparison. Because of this, the stem sheaths are much less important aesthetically. It is really the leaves that have the starring role here, or perhaps the whole aspect: because the stem has three to seven side branches at each node, with their leaves close to the outer end, the whole plant has an exuberantly leafy, somewhat tropical effect in a garden. Although some species – for instance, *Pleioblastus chino* or *P. hindsii* – can grow to a height of a couple of metres, when we think of species from this genus we gen-erally think of dwarves or ground cover. They are not, then, employed in the garden so much as solitaries, but as ground cover or for planting in beds – a use in which rhizome barriers certainly must not be forgotten.

Pleioblastus distichus (synonymous with *P. pygmaeus* var. *distichus*) is one of the smallest bamboos for the garden. Through pruning, which it takes very well, it can be kept quite short, 20 to 40 cm tall. The trimming can even be done with a lawnmower or brushcutter. The leaves are small and green. They are set in two rows and on a plane, and therefore have a feathery appearance. The name distichus refers to this arrangement of leaves (distichus = in two rows). It is an excellent ground cover, spreading vigorously, and loves a place in semi-shade. In certain applications – for instance, small front gardens – it can be a good alternative for a lawn.

Although *Pleioblastus linearis* is not as hardy, in protected spots it will survive winters well. Originally it comes from the Ryukyu Islands in Japan and is one of the larger species in the genus. It can attain a height of over 5 m. It is a very elegant bamboo, with long, slender blades that are almost reminiscent of grass. The whole plant looks like a fantastic plume, and if you have ever seen it in the Fuji Bamboo Garden in Japan, you will never forget it. Like all *Pleioblastus*, it is inclined to spread and thus must be kept reined in. This is a species that one can only really do justice to as a solitary – and then preferably isolated from other planting, for instance in the midst of a lawn.

Pleioblastus variegatus (synonymous with *P. fortunei*) is a low-growing species with variegated foliage, which takes trimming well and thus can be kept at a height of between

30 and 50 cm. This makes it suitable as ground cover and for planting in beds. The leaves have stripes in all tints of green, white and cream. Even in somewhat sunnier areas the colours hold up well, in contrast to many other variegated bamboos. It was introduced to Belgium as early as 1863, from Japan.

Pleioblastus viridistriatus (synonymous with *P. auricomus*) is a beautiful, relatively large species that, if not trimmed, can become 1.5 m tall. However, it accepts an annual pruning very well, so that it can perfectly well be kept at 0.5 m. Pruning also shows the young leaves off all the better. These are variegated, in shades of green and yellow. The name here indeed refers to that quality: *viridistriatus* means 'with green stripes'. The colour contrasts become less pronounced in the older leaves, which is thus a reason for trimming. In the spring it can be pruned back to the ground without worry. That will also enable spectators to enjoy the young shoots, which are first orange and then turn purple-green. It is an outstanding ground cover and very well suited for planting in beds. However, dry ground and very deep shade are to be avoided. Half-shade, for instance under deciduous trees, is fine. The species is adequately hardy for our winters.

Pseudosasa

Pseudosasa is a genus of medium-height to tall Asian bamboos with leptomorphic rhizomes. The best-known species from it is undoubtedly *Pseudosasa japonica*, which in Belgium can still be found in many older gardens. *Pseudosasa japonica* has large, rather showy leaves that can be up to 35 cm long. The stems are straight and reach a height of 4 to 5 m. The side branches are as thick as the stems. It grows diffusely, but in an irregular manner. This makes the plant unpredictable, and a rhizome barrier is therefore advised. The species can be used as an impenetrable, evergreen living partition. Birds love to perch in it, and other small animals enjoy the protection among the stems. It is less interesting as a solitary, and for that use is better replaced by the variety 'Tsutsumiana'.

'Tsutsumiana' is distinguished from the species by its swollen internodes. The sections between the nodes take on a bit of an egg shape. Some effort is needed to enjoy it optimally. The less striking stems – that is, those with less pronounced swellings – should be pruned away, and the stem sheaths, which hide the sight of the swollen base of the internode, should be removed from the whole plant. Otherwise, the general appearance of this variety is similar to that of the species.

(Above) *Pseudosasa japonica* was and is frequently used for its wide leaves on a 4 to 5-m-high plant
(Below) *Pseudosasa japonica* 'Tsutsumiana' has swollen internodes at the bottom of the stem

Sasa

The genus *Sasa* is a taxonomic puzzle. At one time there were more than 400 species counted; according to the latest insights, this number has been reduced to less than 10% of that. But a number of matters are still up for discussion.

Sasa are usually medium-height, very aggressively spreading bamboos with large leaves that are grouped close to the top of the stalks. Its rhizome system is leptomorphic, and the installation of a rhizome barrier at the time of planting is always advised. These species have large leaves set in groups near the apex of the stem. The appearance of only one side branch per node is characteristic. The diameter of this side branch is almost identical to that of the stem. *Sasa* come primarily from Japan, where the plants grow as far north as Sakhalin, which stretches from 45° to 55° northern latitude. That makes *Sasa* the genus with the most northerly distribution. They are also to be found in China and Korea.

Sasa kurilensis is found naturally in the Kuril Islands, northeast of Hokkaido, Japan. They are completely hardy and thrive in cold, wet, snowy conditions. The plants can grow to 1.5 m tall. Their leaves are thick and up to 25 cm long and 7.5 cm wide. The species can also tolerate living in full shadow. With its strong tendency to run, it can be used as ground cover or for planting in beds, or for instance on the edge of a canal or natural pond. For artificial ponds with plastic liners it should only be used in conncection with very efficient rhizome barriers.

Sasa tsuboiana is found more to the south, in central and southern Japan, at altitudes of up to 1250 m. It has striking glossy, dark green leaves that are somewhat larger than those of *S. kurilensis*. This is also true of the size of the plant in general. This species spreads less than, for instance, *S. palmata*, but we would still advise using a rhizome barrier. This species also responds well in shade.

Sasa veitchii is a favourite particularly in wintertime. The edges of the strikingly wide, dark green leaves dry out in that season and give the impression of a white edge. These are not actually variegated leaves, since what is involved is a parchment-like, desiccated section of the leaf blade. The leaves are themselves somewhat smaller than in many other species in this genus, although they can still be 25 cm long and 6 cm wide. It can be employed as ground cover or for planting in beds, and users should not forget the rhizome barrier, because this species does exhibit a capacity to spread vigorously. It grows to be about 1.5 m tall, but can trimmed back in the winter with no adverse effects.

(Above) *Sasa kurilensis* is an outstanding, ever-green ground cover
(Below) The leaves of *Sasa tsuboiana* vary in size. Height, 1 to 2 m

Sasaella

This genus looks like *Sasa*, but has smaller leaves and from one to three side branches per node. It is also a genus from Japan; its distribution range centres on the main island, Honshu. Taxonomically this genus too is a puzzle which has not yet been solved. At the moment there are about a dozen species acknowledged.

Sasaella glabra 'Albostriata' (synonymous with *S. masa mueana* 'Albostriata') is a very attractive bamboo with creamy-white variegated, leathery leaves that can be up to 25 cm long. Particularly in the young leaves, the attractive creamy-white stripes are absolutely worth the gardener's efforts. To do full justice to the variegated character, it is necessary to prune the plants back each spring. The plants grow to about 1.5 m in height and are leptomorphic, which means that a rhizome barrier is advised. It can be used as a solitary, or as ground cover and for planting in beds. The plants accept semi-shade.

We have hesitated to include *Sasaella ramosa*, because this species has an almost uncontrollable habit of spreading. The results of this can be seen in the Kalmthout Arboretum in Belgium, and in Japan the director of the Fuji Bamboo Garden, Haratsugu Kashiwagi, also admits that it is difficult to keep this plant under control. But the enormous inclination to expand its territory can also be an advantage, for instance if it is planted to secure the soil on the slopes of embankments. The leaves are supple and green. The height can reach 1.5 m, but normally the plants remain lower, and they respond well to pruning. They can be mowed in the spring with a brushcutter or even a flail mower. They do require a rather sunny spot to grow.

Semiarundinaria

These bamboos too have leptomorphic rhizomes. They are endemic in Japan and are considered by some authors to be a cross between *Phyllostachys* and *Pleioblastus*. The type for this genus is *S. fastuosa*.

Semiarundinaria fastuosa is the largest species from this genus. Its Dutch name, column bamboo, says something about its manner of growth. The stems are bolt upright, and despite their great height of 8 m or more, hardly bend. In the sun the green stems gradually turn brick-red to purple-brown. A striking characteristic is that the stem sheaths tend to hang onto the stems for a long time after they dry out. The plant produces many side branches and

(Above) Summer appearance of *Sasa veitchii*. In the late autumn and winter the leaves have a decorative white border as a result of drying. Height, 1 to 1.5 m
(Below) *Sasaella glabra* 'Albostriata' has exquisite yellow-white lengthwise stripes on its leaves. Height, 1 to 2 m
p. 92-93: *Semiarundinaria fastuosa* is stiffly erect, reaching 7 m. Private garden, Vlimmeren, Belgium

is quite leafy. It therefore lends itself to use as a screen or high hedge. But it is also well worthwhile as a solitary. In normal conditions it does not have a strong tendency to spread. The variety 'Viridis' is comparable with the species, but the stems and leaves are dark green, and remain so even in the sun. The leaves are slightly smaller, and the plant grows somewhat higher, to about 10 m. It has a stronger tendency to spread than the species, so it must be planted with a rhizome barrier. It works well as a reliable green solitary or as a high partition.

Shibataea

Shibataea are bamboos with leptomorphic rhizomes and generally short stems, with one or two internodes. The nodes on the stems have three to seven side branches, which do not ramify further. There are about ten species known, primarily from eastern China.

Shibataea kumasaca is the best-known species and grows wild in southern Japan. The striking leaves are about 8 cm long and 2.5 cm wide, and appear almost rectangular. They stand on short branches, and the plant itself is very compact. It grows to about 1 m in height. It requires acid soil, because in alkaline soil the leaves scorch. The rhizomes are close to the surface and spread moderately. A rhizome barrier is recommended to make control easier. This is an attractive species with an unmistakable appearance. It is particularly beautiful as a low hedge or partition, but can also be planted in beds.

(Above) *Semiarundinaria fastuosa* is a must for its stem sheaths
(Below) *Semiarundinaria fastuosa* 'Viridis' retains its beautiful dark green colour even in full sun

Shibataea kumasaca differs from other bamboo in the form of its leaves. It is an ideal plant for a border. Height, 1 to 1.5 m

Prafrance: realisation of a bamboo dream

In 1855 Eugène Mazel decided to begin with the most extraordinary project: the creation of a botanical garden devoted to one exceptional plant, bamboo. Here his genius and his dream came together, and he used all the knowledge he had acquired and all the means his time offered. The Bambouseraie was born.

Mazel's success was in part assured by the unusual circumstances of the site of Prafrance. For instance, the soil of the 34 ha large terrain 50 km northeast of Montpellier is alluvial, and both rich and permeable. A nearby river, the Gardon, permitted the construction of a network of canals, good for the permanent irrigation of the whole park. The natural relief forms a bowl, thus creating a very favourable microclimate. The weather, influenced by the Mediterranean Sea climate, provides abundant precipitation (about 1200 mm per year), sometimes as heavy storms (680 mm in ten hours on September 9, 2002). The summers can be very warm, averaging 33 °C. The winters can be rather cold, with temperatures dropping to −19 °C in 1985 and 1986. All these factors were of particular importance in developing this park, with most of its attention devoted to bamboo, but also to such exotics as sequoias, magnolias and palms. At the same time, just outside the park there was a nursery, intended as a place to raise all the necessary species. The history of this nursery therefore runs parallel with that of the park. The interesting bamboos that are raised here for gardens, parks and green zones are divided according to use. *Pleioblastus*, *Sasa* and *Shibataea* are regarded as dwarf bamboos. The small bamboos are *Chimonobambusa*, *Fargesia*, *Hibanobambusa*, *Pleioblastus* and *Sasa*. *Bambusa*, *Chimonobambusa*, *Hibanobambusa*, *Phyllostachys*, *Pseudosasa*, *Pleioblastus* and *Semiarundinaria* are termed the medium-size bamboos. The real giants are *Bambusa* and *Phyllostachys*. In order to prevent bamboos from growing together with one another, it is enough to enclose or deplete them. There are several methods for enclosing them, of which two are widely known and used: the first consists of placing an underground barrier in order to obstruct the further development of the rhizomes, the second of encircling the plant with a ditch about 30 to 40 cm wide and deep. Each winter one must cross this and cut off all the rhizomes which have appeared. To deplete the plants, one cuts off all the unwanted new shoots at the base.

It is necessary to prune bamboos in order to obtain the optimal ornamental effect. Dwarf and low bamboos are pruned at the end of the winter. Medium-sized and giant bamboos should be thinned annually during the winter.

The use of dwarf bamboo in gardening

In Japan dwarf bamboo has been widely used for landscaping for hundreds of years. Most kinds originally come from Japan, and the two most important species belong to the genera *Sasa* and *Pleioblastus*. *Sasa* occurs most frequently in woods and forests, and *Pleioblastus* in open spaces. A number of these species have certain qualities which make them very valuable for use in gardening. Furthermore, many of the Japanese species of bamboos are higly decorative; the rich colour patterns on the leaves and stems make these plant still more attractive for gardeners. The natural distribution of these species is of importance if we want to know about their optimal use in gardens.

Dwarf bamboos are used, first and foremost, as ground cover, for they have the necessary characteristics required of plants employed for this purpose:

– a height of less than 50 cm
– remain green year-round (preferably, but species that lose their leaves once a year can be effective as well)
– provide a compact cover for the soil surface
– grow quickly and have the potential to spread vigorously
– have an effective, widely-spread underground system (roots with rhizomes)
– have attractive foliage with good colour nuances and texture
– be resistant to damage by insects
– require little maintenance.

Although dwarf bamboo has been used as ground cover for centuries in Japan, the methods for planting, the choice of types and even the maintenance are today mostly empirical and rarely scientific. Local climatic conditions in Japan, the structure of the soil, and of course irrigation all influence the speed of growth.
Let us therefore first look at how the different species of dwarf bamboo adapt to the landscape, so that we can see where they can best be planted in a garden.

Influence of seasonal changes on growth

The rootstocks of the different species grow very well during the hot and dry summer months, except for those of *Sasa*. The most vigorous spreading of the rootstocks is found in *Pleioblastus*. The stems of some *Sasa* and *Sasaella* species have a short life span. The stems of *Pleioblastus* and *Shibataea* species, however, have a relatively longer life span. The number of leaves on *Pleioblastus* and *Sasaella* differ sharply from season to season, but the foliage of *Pleioblastus* often suffers in the winter months (various kinds of *Pleioblastus* do not remain green during the winter). *Sasa* and *Shibataea* have about the same number of leaves all year round. The individual leaves of all species have a life span of about one year.

Adaptation to varying environments

Pleioblastus species can easily adapt to various environments and circumstances, world-wide. *Shibataea kumasaca* and *Sasaella kogasensis* var. *Gracillima* display a relatively strong resistance against dry soils and various soil compositions, and grow very well in strong light. They tolerate shade well, but the number of leaves diminishes in darker situations. Moreover, they lose their compact shape and take on a more open form of growth. *Shibataea kumasaca* and *Sasaella* species can adapt to diverse soil conditions, and grow well under open or slightly shaded conditions. Although *Shibataea* kumasaca does grow larger in darker conditions, its ornamental value is diminished by the fact that the number of leaves reduces itself through seasonal changes. In the *Sasa* group the capacity to adapt to soil conditions varies from species to species. *Sasa veitchii* prefers rich soils with very good water retention. This species has a superior toleration for shade and retains the same number of leaves under similar, though darker conditions.

Maintenance of dwarf bamboos

The maintenance of dwarf bamboos focuses primarily on fertilisation, pruning and watering. For several years after planting it is necessary to fertilise them well, but this is no longer required once the plant is full-grown. Instead, it becomes important to control the growth by means of pruning. By cutting back the plant, the old stems are removed and inordinate growth is limited. Pruning is most effective in the genus *Pleioblastus*. Many *Pleioblastus* lose their strength and attractiveness if they are not cut back, and therefore the plant is shown off to its best advantage by regular pruning. In normal circumstances, the pruning should be done around the middle of March, which conforms with the growth rhythm of the dwarf bamboo. There are however certain cases in which the growth must be controlled stronger and in which other pruning schedules and intensities must be considered. In order to obtain a larger number of leaves on *Pleioblastus*, or to limit the height of the stems, pruning must also be done in the autumn.

p.98-99: Because of its spreading growth, *Sasaella ramosa* is ideal for large areas

Cutting in the middle of the stems speeds up branching, because this stimulates the hidden buds at the nodes on the stalks. This provides for a thicker, more compact plant.

Use of dwarf bamboo in landscape architecture

All this information is very useful for employing dwarf bamboo in large gardens and parks. *Pleioblastus* species are extraordinarily suited for use in landscape gardens that change enormously through the four seasons, in places that are rather dry, and even on a larger scale as a massive ground cover; they can be freely trimmed according to the purpose. In these species, pruning in the late winter assures that the fresh, green leaves rejuvenate the plant, and that the desiccated winter appearance is replaced by luxuriant spring growth. Moreover, the pruning can be drastic in order to achieve this. *Sasa* species grow very well in deep shadow and adapt to relatively damp areas in forest soils, etc. They do not really like pruning and require special care. For instance, if *Sasa* is selected as ground cover for open spots without irrigation, it will have problems during dry and warm periods, and the leaf cover can dry out and die back. If these leaves are cut back, the plant will only restore itself slowly. *Sasa* bamboos are better suited for shaded areas of a garden, among woody plants which provide shadow and protection. *Shibataea* is suited for introducing green into open spaces in large areas and in scattered, woody soils. The height of the stems can be freely controlled by pruning. *Sasaella* species can be used in the same manner as *Shibataea*, but are less tolerant of pruning, as it takes longer to create a thick number of leaves. As with other plants, when it comes to evaluating their serviceability in a landscape, it is important to know the native habitat of each sort of dwarf bamboo in order to find the most efficient use for its aesthetic attraction and success as ground cover.

Any botanically interested observer walking through the woods in Japan will see various species of *Sasa* that thrive luxuriantly as giant grasses in the shadow of *Cryptomeria* and *Acer* and *Ilex*. If that observer rides through open grassland, a sign alongside the road may tell him that the meadows are completely covered by *Pleioblastus*. In Japan, dwarf bamboo is present everywhere in the wild. And those who then visit the splendidly maintained gardens of Kyoto in Japan will understand the use of dwarf bamboo and its potential in landscapes world-wide.

Pleioblastus pygmaeus is a low-maintenance alternative for the traditional ornamental lawn

Applications

Architecture

From time immemorial mankind has used bamboo in the construction of his dwellings. The advantages of this rectilinear material were discovered early: it grows and replenishes itself rapidly, and can be worked and shaped with a simple knife. Quite early too man discovered the structural carrying capacity of this hollow material, an amazing form of natural technology. Well before the bronze and iron ages men had realised that the long fibres of this plant, which are rich in silicon dioxide, make it a true vegetable form of steel. This insight and understanding of this exceptional product has led to both the experimental constructions one finds in native dwellings in traditional Asian and African cultures, and to the consciously planned, yet inspired and lyrical modernism of Colombian and Japanese architects.

It is the versatility of this vegetable giant, a mixture of strength and suppleness, sturdiness and subtlety, plastic qualities and adaptability, that in all ages has made bamboo a material for the future. It is no wonder that this material has always fascinated architects; among them in our time such masters of the craft as Buckminster Fuller, Frei Otto, Renzo Piano, Shoei Yoh, Oscar Hidalgo and Simón Vélez.

This latter is rightly called the pope of bamboo architecture for the spectacular and detailed form of his realisations. We need merely think of the pavilion of the Swiss environmental foundation ZERI that was made for the World Exposition in Hanover in 2000: with a roof 40 m in diameter, supported by 20 pillars 14 m high, it is a vegetable cathedral of 3500 sticks of *Guadua angustifolia*. Despite its complete European modernity, this construction could certainly have counted on the admiration of the great medieval master builders. The gigantic roof of the Penalisa golf club in Girardot, Colombia, is without doubt the largest construction in bamboo today. Behind this project, which some regard as too flamboyant, there is an indisputable savoir faire that can accomplish a true symbolic revolution, namely the rise of a 'cultivatable architecture'. To speak of bamboo in such terms is not an exaggeration. The rapid growth of this plant makes it possible to cultivate and exploit it by means of plantations without damaging the environment. In sharp contrast to this, a tree is destroyed in the moment of its felling, something that is absolutely not desirable in this world in which people are desperately searching for fibre-rich materials from nature. Wise farmers in Asia, Africa and Latin America have always made sure that there is a clump of bamboo near their dwelling. Thus they continually had an outstanding natural

construction material within reach. It is this well-managed availability that has permitted them, after manifold experimentation, to create an inventive form of architecture which is perfectly adapted to its environment. One experiences this clearly when one discovers the dazzling harmony of the woven walls of the fishermen's huts on Lake Inle in Iwama in Myanmar (Burma). Another such instance is the unbelievable accumulation of bamboo for the construction of the roofs of the Tongkoman, the traditional houses in the land of Toraja (Celebes, Indonesia), or again, the sumptuous bamboo ornamental leaf work for the roofs of the pavilions in Balinese temples.

These numerous realisations open the book on human creativity. It is precisely from them that contemporary architects and designers like Linda Garland and Marcello Villegas, or artists like Hiroshi Teshigahara draw their inspiration and the magic of their projections. And it is in that context that the idea arose of using bamboo to make modern materials from it that inspire a new natural architecture: bamboo parquet, beams, corrugated bamboo sheets, woven screens ...

These new developments in the architectural use of bamboo likewise inspired Kengo Kuma and his 'digital bamboo', or the woven structure of the Naiju Community Centre at Chikuko, Fukuoka, Japan, from the hand of Shoei Yoh, or again the temporary pavilion by Rocco Yim for the Berlin "Festival of Vision" in 2000. In every age bamboo has made an essential contribution to the evolution of architecture.

Today bamboo is still the model for the highest human structures: young bamboo shoots suggested the shape of the two gigantic Petronas Towers in Kuala Lumpur, and an adult bamboo inspired the figure of the new apartment highrise of 501 m in Taipeh, Taiwan. It is not for nothing that in a number of Asian enterprises the legend of their origin takes the form of a bamboo, as if it were a sort of matrix architecture for a company.

Treating the ends of fresh stalks

Fungus at the base of a stem

Protecting bamboo against degeneration

The bamboo stalk is an essential construction material that is used in countless applications. In bamboo-growing countries it is increasingly used as a replacement for wood, a tendency encouraged by the shortage of timber. In the Western world too bamboo is being used as a building material, as for instance in the ZERI Pavilion at EXPO 2000 in Hanover, or an open-air pavilion in Vergiate in northern Italy, or for a bridge in the vicinity of Amsterdam. There are various reasons for the rising interest in bamboo. Bamboo structures not only have a certain elegance, but bamboo can also be used to create an exotic look, as it does for a car park at the zoo in Leipzig. Its general acceptance is limited, however, by the fact that the material is relatively susceptible to biological deterioration, including bamboo structural elements and finished products. In certain environments bamboo is easily attacked by beetles and fungus. If bamboo constructions come into contact with soil, they will be destroyed within two years. With the right protection, the life span of constructions can be extended to four to seven years; some applications in protected conditions, such as bamboo parquet, can last much longer. In contrast to hard woods from many trees that produce poisonous substances which repel fungus and insects, bamboo stalks have no similar deterrence system, so that the whole fabric can be destroyed and only the hard outer shell remains.

The susceptibility to boring insects and blue fungus is explained by the presence of starch, a principle food source (see page 25). For their enzyme action, fungi need sufficient water and air. Because of this, both water-saturated and air-dried bamboo stalks are naturally protected against normal fungi. Structural methods that keep bamboo dry or avoid contact with damp as much as possible are very efficient against fungi. The bamboo-boring insects widespread in the tropics degrade the fabric of the stalk through their gnawing larvae. Small piles of dust from their boring are immediate indications of the destruction, and small holes show where the beetles have crawled out in search of partners or to lay their eggs. In European climatic conditions, fungi are more of a threat than beetles.

The prevention of biological damage is more difficult with bamboo than for various kinds of wood. Since most bamboo for construction must be imported, in general one cannot select the stalks oneself, and quality is thus not always guaranteed. Stems must be older than three years (adult) and harvested after the new young shoots have appeared on the same plant, because that will have reduced the starch content in the stems themselves. There is no other way to control the amount of starch in the stems. Preferably, the stalks must be conserved at their place of origin. Any treatment must take place while the stalks are still fresh, since treatment later becomes more difficult.

There are various methods of treatment. Almost all the methods utilise toxic chemicals. Until recently the possible effects on mammals and the environment where hardly taken into account. Currently the laws and regulations are much stronger and this will influence the customary methods, which are still dangerous. Alternatives are being considered, such as the traditional smoking, which is being further developed in Colombia. This method was used for the bamboo in the EXPO Pavilion, but because of the contractual obligation to tear down the whole structure after the exhibition, the long-term efficiency of this method could not be tested there. A similar structure in Pereira, Colombia, will however provide such information.

Treating the stalks with chemical solutions means that these must be able to get into the tissue. As indicated on page 24, the outside of the stalk is however protected by an impervious layer which prevents the water-based solutions with the protective chemicals from getting inside the stalk. Therefore liquids can only reach the inside of the stalk if they enter from the two ends, and move through the tracheae. Since the tracheae only make up 6 to 8% of the entire tissue, the liquid must spread further through the surrounding tissue to fully protect the stalk. In general, salts based on boric acid are used. They spread easily, but almost never stick, so care must be taken that the stalks never become wet again.

The treatment method employed depends on the purpose for which the plant will be used, the type of material (round or split) and aspects relating to the environment. For fresh stalks, replacement of the internal plant sap is the most suitable treatment, a method that was developed by A. Boucherie in 1840 for treating spruce. The preservative is pushed into one end of the stem, replaces the sap of the plant, and flows out again at the other end. With the preservative spreading thoughout the stem, the stalks are completely treated without anything coming into contact with the surface, as is the case with other methods. For bamboo canes or supports for fruit trees, this method is employed as a simple procedure for which no special requisites are necessary: the bottoms of the fresh stalks are placed in a container and the preservative penetrates them through the end by absorption and capillary action.

Another method often used is letting the stalks soak in a bath. In order to encourage the absorption, small holes must be made in the septa that are found at the nodes in every bamboo stem. These can be punctured by a long iron rod. Split bamboo and matting are also treated in this manner.

The pressure method, another technique for impregnating bamboo stalks, provides the best long-term protection, but is seldom used. It demands expensive technical installations, special treatment, and there must be sufficient economic demand. As it happens, the side-effects for the environment are considerable.

Air-dried bamboo does not easily absorb water, unless the bottom of the stalk stands directly in damp soil or water. In this same manner, however, the bottom of the stem can be protected if it is immersed in a protective liquid. Painting the outside of bamboo for protection makes no sense at all, since the liquid just runs off the waxy surface, causing contamination to the soil.

The use of protective chemicals for bamboo and the use of the treated products – the remains of which will be consigned to rubbish tips – pose possible indirect risks for people and the environment. The treatment should only be done in places where there is sufficient knowledge, experience and control on hand. Preferably, bamboo should be treated at its place of origin. Before being transported the stems must be air-dried in order to resist fungal infection during shipping in containers.

For bamboo grown in Europe no chemical protection is used, with the exception of random home treatments. For weighing the possible risks against the benefits an expert should be consulted.

Even in bamboo-growing countries its inclination to degradation and problems with the proper protection are leading to increasing competition from, or replacement of bamboo by plastics. In some places such 'original bamboo imitations' are cheaper, longer-lasting (with a guarantee) – and available in different colours.

Partition of real bamboo,
and plastic imitation bamboo

Sap replacement treatment for fresh stalks

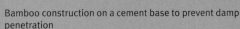

Bamboo construction on a cement base to prevent damp penetration

Industry

When European consumers think of bamboo products, generally the very first associations are traditional applications such as basketwork and handcrafts. A typical instance is rustic bamboo furniture that displays the characteristic divisions of the stalks, or charming bamboo houses with thatched roofs that remind one of idyllic images of tropical destinations. Indeed, many Europeans think of bamboo as belonging to the East. Although there is nothing wrong with that, it is important to realise that bamboo is much more than a prop piece for a sunny vacation.

Bamboo is really an extraordinary material with unique chemical and mechanical properties. It brightens up our world, both symbolically and literally: Thomas Edison used bamboo fibres in his first incandescent lamps. And as the fastest growing woody plant, bamboo is a hope for a renewable source of timber for industrial applications.

Anyone who ever takes a real tour around a bustling Asian city, or a virtual internet tour of any place from Hanoi to Hong Kong, will unavoidably come face to face with bamboo in the service of industry. The sight of humble bamboo constructions against impressive skyscrapers confirms the role of bamboo in modern construction projects. In contemporary applications the hollow, tubular form of bamboo is not always present. Attentive observers, however, will discover that the fine parquet on which they stand and the luxurious ceiling over their heads are not made from trees, but from processed bamboo. If one looks closely enough, bamboo can be seen everywhere, from matchsticks and toothpicks to paper products and

medicines. It is used for coffee filters and is possibly even present in the fibres of the upholstery in your automobile. It is used to make pallets, container floors or decking for lorries and ships. It is used as wood in construction and is processed into the strong paper bags for cement. Bamboo is also processed to become fine writing paper and is in pencils. And if you go to a Chinese restaurant, you can eat bamboo shoots with bamboo chopsticks, and the fish on your plate may have been caught in a bamboo trap, and grilled on bamboo charcoal.

Bamboo is an old resource with uncounted uses, but it is relatively new as an industrial material. The exploitation and use of bamboo for industrial mass production began in the 20th century. Before 1920 bamboo was recognised as a high-quality fibre which could replace wood in the making of paper. Of course, the Chinese had used bamboo

to make paper for more than 1800 years, but it was only under the colonial domination of Britain that pulp and paper mills in India began to use modern, mechanised methods for the production of 100% bamboo paper. Since then, every region with bamboo has gradually adopted this plant as the most important source for fibre and wood for industrial applications. With a steady supply of bamboo at its disposal, China took the initiative in developing innovative panel products from bamboo. The introduction of flat bamboo panels and parquet flooring by Chinese factories was an important evolution in both local and export markets. By 1990 the attractiveness of bamboo had taken on global proportions, and bamboo products became more and more common in European and American markets. Advances driven by the development of innovative wood products are an ongoing process, and gradually bamboo was used to make chipboard and fibreboard.

Although China remains the primary source of such modern industrially produced goods, the level of bamboo use in many other countries has developed from the traditional craftwork to mass produced industrial products too. In India various innovative products are being developed, including woven bamboo mats processed into hard sheets, corrugated sheets and fibreboard and chipboard. There is also increased interest in bamboo in South America, and in Europe there is ongoing research being done into advanced bamboo applications.

Another sector associated with bamboo is the food processing industry. Bamboo food products fall into two general groups: bamboo drinks and bamboo shoots. Bamboo drinks come in alcoholic and non-alcoholic varieties. The alcoholic drinks include bamboo beer, which is brewed and bottled in China, and bamboo wine, the fer-mented sap of an African species, *Oxytenanthera braunii*, which is produced and consumed principally in Tanzania. Bamboo beer is actually an ordinary hop beer that is mixed with an extract from bamboo leaves. Medicinal qualities are attributed to it, as a pick-me-up. Non-alcoholic bamboo drinks are limited to bamboo sap made from bamboo leaves. Bottled bamboo beer and canned bamboo sap are sold in China and Hong Kong. Such drinks will have less of an attraction on the Western market, but the niche market in China alone already supports an industry that is worth many millions of euros.

Bamboo shoots are an important industry world-wide. Bamboo shoots are vegetables; they are the young sprouts of the plant, and are harvested within a week after they have appeared above ground. Anyone who has eaten at a Chinese restaurant will most likely have already tasted bamboo shoots, and has thus contributed to supporting an industry that brings in billions of euros. Bamboo shoots are a basic ingredient in Eastern cuisine. At their best, they are crunchy and have a sweet taste. The constant demand for bamboo shoots, combined with their perishability in shops means that top quality products can often be exported for colossal sums. The bamboo shoots that are consumed in Western Europe are normally canned, primarily imported from China and Thailand. Shoots that are raised in China come principally from the species *Phyllostachys edulis*, which received its name from the fact that the shoots can be eaten. In Thailand the *Dendrocalamus asper,* a giant pachymorphic bamboo, is the primary source for the shoots. Commercial plantations of *Dendrocalamus asper* are famous for their annual production of more than 10 tonnes of fresh bamboo shoots per hectare. Plantations that are devoted to the production of bamboo shoots represent a lucrative business in places where distribution and marketing channels are well developed.

Bamboo represents an alternative for timber for the panel and plank industry. This industry produces a wide variety of products, running from laminated planks to fibreboard and chipboard, which in turn form the basic materials for furniture and decorative panels. Bamboo's biology and anatomical structure provides many advantages over wood, but one of its shortcomings is its high volume-to-weight ratio. With the exception of several massive or half-massive species, bamboos are hollow, and road transport is not economical. Processing bamboo into flat sheets solves this problem, and makes it practical to transport it with other materials. Bamboo sheets and laminates have still other plus-points that make them a worthy alternative to wood. With regard to elasticity, various laboratory tests have shown that bamboo performs better than steel. Bamboo is very resistant to blows and as hard as oak. Its strength is a key to its success as a much-in-demand flooring product. Bamboo parquet is produced primarily in China, although there are such factories to be found in other parts of the world, including Latin American countries such as Ecuador and Colombia. Chinese bamboo parquet is made principally from the stems of the Moso bamboo, the popular name of *Phyllostachys edulis*. In Latin America, parquet boards are made from the *Guadua angustifolia*, while in the Philippines they are made from *Bambusa blumeana*, a thorny, clump-forming bamboo.

The process of making bamboo flooring involves several steps. First the bamboo is split into strips lengthwise. After that, the cane is flattened and the curved walls are changed into flat strips. During this process the thickness of each bamboo strip is reduced from 12 mm to 7 mm. The process of rolling and flattening results in a huge amount of waste. Many of the factories in China use the sawdust and chips to generate the energy necessary for the various stages in the production. For instance, power is needed to heat the boiler in which the flat bamboo strips are immersed to bleach or preserve them. The bamboo strips are then placed in a lime kiln in which they are dried over several days at a low temperature. Once they are dried, the bamboo strips are once again rolled to a thickness of 6 mm. They are then glued together with a methanal-based resin and compressed to form sheets which are cut into standard lengths. The sheets are next milled with a tongue-and-groove cutter, and then sanded smooth and polished. Finally, various finishing touches can be added and treatments carried out, including uv painting.

Some factories give the sheets a coat of stained lacquer, while others deliver them without additional finishing layers, and leave it to the consumer to choose the final colour.

When one considers the scarcity of hard wood resources, bamboo panels and sheets stand out head and shoulders as an environmentally friendly product, for bamboo rapidly replenishes itself and is easily recycled. Thus it is no surprise that bamboo has an implicit approval from the *United Nations Environmental Programme*, whose offices in Washington, D.C., have bamboo floors. But aside from the ecological arguments, bamboo still stands out as a viable alternative for wood parquet through its unique charm and unmistakable character. In Europe and North America bamboo is increasingly making a name for itself as a material of choice for interior designers. Private businesses and governmental offices are choosing bamboo with increasing frequency as a warm and elegant material for interiors. A striking example is the international airport in Madrid, where bamboo panels were used as a ceiling in the new terminal.

In India the search for inexpensive building materials for the mass market has led to the development of hardened bamboo mats. These hard mats are the ultimate combination of tradition and modernity, of craftwork with industrial refinement. The basic materials are the traditional mats that are hand-woven from bamboo slivers by women in rural areas. The woven mats are further processed in a modern factory where they are immersed in an adapted carbolic acid-methanal resin, mixed with a preservative to better protect the mats against termites and rotting. The mats, which are directly covered with a layer of resin, are then dried in tunnels with hot steam. They are next assembled into layers at right angles to one another, ten to fifteen layers thick, and then pressed together under heat to create multiplex bamboo mats of the desired thickness. As a finishing touch, the sides of the sheets are covered with a veneer or resin-permeated paper, and again compressed under heat to make a strong panel that looks like wood.

The process of making these sheets is also applied to make bamboo-mat corrugated roof panels. The major difference lies in the sort of press used, which creates the ribbed form of the panel. In many developing countries, where asbestos roofs are still used, this roofing material from bamboo is an inexpensive and – more importantly – a non-cancer causing alternative for the mass market.

The rise of bamboo panel products has had a strong impact on the bamboo furniture sector. Much of the bamboo furniture from China is no longer recognisable as a bamboo product. The curves have disappeared and been replaced by angles. The material has undergone a complete metamorphosis and has been totally reworked. If the material retains its natural colour, then the fine grain and gnarled stripes will still clearly refer to the original material. All in all, the use of bamboo in modern furniture is an important step in the direction of ecological functionality. Traditional bamboo furniture is very clumsy and not very practical for today's houses. By contrast, the new stream-lined tables, chairs and beds from bamboo are much better suited for modern homes.

Without doubt, bamboo has achieved spectacular successes as a raw material for large industry. Many manufacturers are following this trend and beginning to develop more products, and in the years to come we can expect still more growth from the processing industry. However, it is of essential importance that the growth of the bamboo industry be accompanied with a parallel growth in commercial bamboo plantations. There are no new plantations being developed any more at the rate that is necessary to assure the required supply for future developments. Most of the bamboo that is being used for industry is still being taken from natural forests. In many areas the cutting of bamboo is not regulated and the implementation of reforestation programmes is very slow. Very often there is shameless over-exploitation, which damages the environment and deprives the rural population of an important source of income. Some species of bamboo have been so over-exploited that they are approaching extinction, and in many places wild animals are paying the price for the destruction of their habitat. So long as bamboo and other forest products can be randomly despoiled there is a great danger that the sources of raw materials for industry will suddenly become insufficient. Fortunately there is a growing awareness of this among international organisations and environmental bodies. The future therefore looks somewhat more optimistic.

In order to preserve the bamboo industry it is necessary to begin with the development of industrial agriculture. That means developing plant nurseries and distributing high-quality plant materials. That also means the development of professionally managed bamboo plantations, which will generate higher profits than natural forests. It also implies using adequate storage and preservation techniques in order to guarantee higher quality in the raw materials, and thus limit waste. Furthermore, it also entails that the factories at the plantations must be connected by creating a marketing and distribution network that assures a win-win situation for the farms and factories. The ultimate winner will be the client, who will have the best product for the best price, but not at the expense of the environment.

p. 116-117: Rafts on the Li river, Yangshuo, China

Music

Wherever bamboo is grown, there is bamboo music. The bamboo stalk is a natural instrument, a woodwind instrument par excellence. Since time immemorial people have used the stem of a bamboo and their breath to produce a melancholy song from nature.

There are hundreds of bamboo instruments, the most popular being the wind instruments, and in particular the flute, and percussion instruments such as marimbas and xylophones. Bamboo wind instruments are made by removing the nodes, which lie at a short distance from each other, in order to produce a completely hollow tube.

Innovations in processing bamboo have created the possibility of using bamboo to make instruments that previously have been made of wood. A familiar example is the acoustic guitar made of bamboo, produced by the Yamaha Corporation. It is a quality instrument with a bright sound and a reasonable price tag. Yamaha also produces snare drums from bamboo. Other innovative instrument makers have produced instruments such as bamboo saxophones, with interesting acoustic results.

Bamboo has withstood the test of time in the musical arena. Traditional instruments from thousands of years ago have survived to today. The concept of panpipes, for instance, is based on the intuitive concept of tube lengths and pitch. They can be made with simple tools, and are relatively easy to play – but very difficult to master completely! Panpipes are apparently the oldest musical instrument, dating from 6000 years ago; they derive their name from Pan, the Greek god of nature, who, according to legend, made these flutes from broken reed stems. The Greek form of this instrument was imitated in countries all over the world, without any historical or cultural connections. The oldest known bamboo flute was played in China, 2500 years ago. The instrument, known as a *pai xiao*, was made from thirteen bamboo tubes tied together with rope. The instrument produced a deep, melancholy sound, which is said to have thrown the philosopher Confucius into a deep depression.

In some cultures, bamboo flutes are associated with religion. In Hinduism and Buddhism the sound of the bamboo flute is less familiar in terms of musical performance, but is used for religious meditation. The *bansuri* bamboo flute, a soprano flute of two octaves, is one of the oldest musical instruments of India. The name *bansuri* is derived from the Sanskrit words *bans*, which means bamboo, and *swar*, which means musical note. The *bansuri* has a strong link with the Vedas and is held horizontally, as you can see in representations of Lord Krishna. For popular music in India the *bansuri* remains a favourite instrument to this day; but recently it has been used for classical music as well.

Japan's best-known woodwind instrument is the *shakuhachi* bamboo flute. The name of the instrument is derived from its standard length of one foot (*shaku*) and eight (*hachi*) parts of a foot (called *sun*), about 55 cm. Playing the *shakuhachi* is known as 'the art of Zen blowing', and is practised by Buddhist monks. It is a meditative art because of the pure, unalloyed sound of the bamboo flute. The gripping tones of the bamboo are intended to take one into deep meditation, in order to make the mind one with nature.

Among the traditional instruments of Bali is the *suling*, a bamboo flute that looks very much like a recorder and is played to accompany Hindu rituals. The *suling* is for Bali what the *bansuri* is for India. It is also present on Java, and in Indonesia is the only melodic woodwind instrument in the *gamelan* orchestra, which is based overwhelmingly on percussion.

Long before the tradition of ensemble music had developed in the West, the people of Asia were playing music in groups with bamboo instruments. One of the oldest ensemble instruments is a sort of rattle which in Indonesia is known as a *angklung*. The instrument is made of two or three vertical bamboo tubes, which are tuned in octaves and attached to a horizontal bamboo stick that is held in the hand. As the instrument is shaken, the tubes slide along the grooves that are cut into the rectangular frame and strike against a bamboo edge, whereupon they produce a reverberating sound. The *angklung* is a monotone instrument, which means that it can produce only one note. In order to play *angklung* music it is thus necessary to form an ensemble, in which each musician plays one note, according to the instrument he has in his hand. In *angklung* the emphasis is on total co-operation and co-ordination, rather than on individual virtuosity.

One of the crown jewels of bamboo music is the unique bamboo organ in the church at Las Piñas. The organ is one of the national treasures of the Philippines. It was built between 1916 and 1921 by Father Diego Cera, the parish priest and an experienced organ builder. Before that he had already used bamboo for components in other organs that he had built in Manila. He then decided to build an organ which was made entirely of bamboo, a material which grew everywhere around Las Piñas. The organ is comprised of 909 bamboo pipes and 122 horizontal metal trumpets that were added later. Natural disasters such as earthquakes and tropical storms damaged both the church and the organ, so that for many years it could no longer be played. In 1973 it was dismantled piece by piece and sent to Germany, where it was restored to its full glory by Johannes Klais Orgelbau in Bonn. Since 1975 Las Piñas has become a pilgrimage site for organists from all over the world, and organ virtuosi do homage to the instrument during the annual International Bamboo Organ Festival. Every spring, as the bamboo in the fields springs into bloom, the bamboo organ pipes of Las Piñas sing their praises in the immortal sounds of Pachelbel, Couperin, Handel and Bach.

Gastronomy

Bamboo is used in Asian cuisine in various ways. Not only are cooking and table utensils made from it – from steaming baskets to chopsticks – but the plant itself is also eaten. Bamboo shoots are one of the most popular vegetables in China, Korea, Japan and the countries of Southeast Asia.

Fresh shoots are most highly valued, but in Myanmar (Burma), for instance, pickled bamboo shoots are considered a delicacy. In China, Korea and Japan the bamboo shoot is symbolic of the spring. Particularly in Japan, where the seasons are strongly reflected in the cuisine, bamboo plays a starring role in April and May.

Shoots which are dug up fresh in the early morning are best if they are eaten the same day. After peeling, they can be used without further processing as ingredients in various dishes. Those lucky individuals who have bamboo in their own garden can enjoy the refined, somewhat sweet taste of this treat to their heart's content. Unfortunately, it is not possible to bring such a fresh product to the markets in urban areas inexpensively. Generally more than 24 hours have passed between the moment when the shoots were dug and the time they reach consumers. As time passes the vegetable takes on a bitter taste, and therefore must first be cooked before it can be used further.

For convenience, bamboo shoots in Asia are often sold already cooked, generally peeled, but sometimes just as they came out of the ground, with many layers of brown skin. After peeling, about half the shoot is left.

In Europe it is unfortunately extremely difficult to find fresh cooked bamboo shoots. We are thus forced to fall back on canned bamboo shoots, the taste of which can hardly be compared with the fresh product. We encounter them for instance in Chinese restaurants, where small slivers of the shoots are stir-fried with vegetables and meat. Cans with cooked strips are also a form in which bamboo shoots are most frequently found on the European market. However, one is advised to search out cans with large pieces rather than the strips, because in terms of taste these are closer to fresh bamboo. A thorough washing, briefly blanching the shoot in hot water and rinsing it in cold water helps to get rid of the bitter aftertaste of canned bamboo.

Filled green bamboo on ice

Bamboo rice (a Japanese recipe)

Ingredients:
1 medium-sized bamboo shoot (about 250 grams)
250 grams chicken (preferably from the thigh)
450 grams Japanese rice (sushi rice), washed
1 litre chicken bouillon
1 teaspoon salt
2 tablespoons Japanese soy sauce
2 tablespoons saki
1/2 leaf nori seaweed

Preparation:
Cut the bamboo shoot in half lengthwise (canned shoots are generally already cut in half) and wash it well. Slice it and wash one more time. Blanch the slices in hot water for one minute and rinse immediately with cold water. Pat dry with a paper towel.

Cut the chicken into cubes of about 1.5 cm and handle them as you did the bamboo shoots – blanch in hot water for one minute, rinse immediately with cold water, and pat dry with a kitchen towel.

Wash the rice and place it in a rice cooker. Mix the bouillon with the salt, soy sauce and sake and pour it over the rice. Add the bamboo shoots and chicken, stir well, and turn on the rice cooker.

If you do not have a rice cooker available, use a heavy pan with a tight-fitting lid. Put the lid on tightly and bring the mixture to the boil over medium heat. Once it boils, increase the heat and cook until almost all the moisture has been absorbed by the rice. Then let the whole continue to cook for 10 minutes over very low heat. Remove the pan from the heat and put it on a tea towel for another 10 to 15 minutes, keeping the lid on.

Free up the bamboo rice carefully with a wooden spoon and serve it into dishes. Just before serving sprinkle the rice with broken, grilled nori seaweed.

Bamboo salad (a 'fusion' recipe)

Ingredients:
1/2 bamboo shoot (about 100 grams)
50 grams watercress
2 tablespoons olive oil
1/2 tablespoon Japanese soy sauce
1/2 teaspoon rasped ginger root

Preparation:
Wash and dry the bamboo shoot, and cut it into flat pieces, not too small. Blanch the pieces in hot water for one minute and wash them immediately with cold water. Pat dry with a paper towel.

Grill the shoots in a grill pan coated with half the olive oil.

While still hot, place the grilled shoots in a bowl with the mixture of the rest of the olive oil, soy sauce and rasped ginger root.

Cut the watercress into large pieces and add it to the cooled bamboo shoots. Mix everything well.

New Year's dishes in Kadomatsu.

Bamboo filled with soft and fresh watery *an*

Florian Seyd

Floristics

Up to now, bamboo has played little role in flower arranging in our culture. Bamboo does not grow naturally in Europe, and it has only been since the 1970s that it has been found more and more in modern gardens. In the meantime, new species which were better suited for our climate were imported from the colder regions and mountains of Asia. European interest for Asian culture in general – food, lifestyle, garden design and plants – has also meant that bamboo is more 'in'.

Thus there is a growing interest in bamboo in floristry. First it was chiefly dried bamboo sticks that arrived in Europe by container. Particularly during the ikebana rage of the 1970s these were much desired by florists. Recently more and more green bamboo stalks from southern Europe (*Phyllostachys edulis* and *Phyllostachys bambusoides*) have been coming in to the flower markets. Products such as dried bamboo leaves, the dried shoot leaf of the *Dendrocalamus* species, and rootstocks with a piece of stem in dried form have become available. But these products are still rather new and do not have any regular place in our floristry.

In Asian floristry bamboo has an established meaning, it is the symbol for life: it is strong but yielding; in a heavy storm the stalks bend supply and immediately after the storm stand straight again. These qualities are considered a model for human behavior. Bamboo is a material around which a great deal of Asian life revolves. In primitive areas it is omnipresent: the houses are built of bamboo, water is carried and cooking is done in bamboo pots, fruit is collected and kept in bamboo baskets of one sort, and animals transported in another, mats are woven from it on which to sleep, bamboo shoots are eaten, and bamboo is used for rituals and traditional celebrations.

Furthermore, bamboo has a prominent role in both traditional and modern ikebana. In Japan bamboo is present from the beginning to the end of their new year's festivities. Every house is decorated with flower arrangements that include bamboo, *pinus* and other floral materials, and accompany this celebration.

The powerful aura of bamboo is used in various ways in floral arrangements. Bamboo is worked into baskets and dishes, and the stems themselves are used as vases. In recent years bamboo has been seen in many large installations. Through centuries of tradition and experience with bamboo, the handling of this material is at an exceptionally high level in Asia.

Since he was seventeen, master florist Florian Seyd has been deeply interested in bamboo. While on vacation he visited Wolfgang Eberts's bamboo nursery in Baden-Baden, Germany, and bought the first bamboo plant for the garden. During his training as a florist his fascination with bamboo only increased. Lessons and demonstrations in Taiwan, where bamboo is a much-used material, spurred him on to try new things with bamboo.

Florian Seyd decided to use bamboo in all possible forms in floral compositions. He has spearheaded efforts to get a wider selection of fresh bamboo products on the European market, and to enrich floristry by designing various structures with bamboo. As a material, bamboo is ready for the future: it grows quickly, can be cultivated well, has a modern aura and is environmentally friendly.

To the question of when his 'calling' as a florist became clear, Florian Seyd answered spontaneously, 'I've really always been involved with flowers, from the time I was a child.' Nature fascinated him, but particularly plants and flowers. As the Seyd family lived in a house in Essen without a garden, it was somewhat difficult to indulge his passion there. He was delighted when they moved to Nordenham and he could have a small garden. This garden was always kept in first-class condition. From the time he was twelve he could help out in a florist's shop after school. He enjoyed himself so much that he spent more and more time there, learning the basic techniques of floristry.

After finishing school and completing two years of an alternative national service – during which he worked in nature conservancy – he decided to continue with floristry. For a couple of years Florian Seyd trained with Gregor Lersch in Bad Neuenahr. He widened his experience considerably and learned to know the world of floristry from the inside. Floral demonstrations in Taiwan, in Switzerland by Nicole von Boletzky, and in many other countries opened up new perspectives, among them on new ways to use bamboo.

Since 1998 he has worked in The Netherlands with Menno Kroon, where he became manager in 2000, with responsibility for the purchase of cut flowers and plants. Since August 1, 2004, he has had his own business.

Philosophy

Bamboo has an important place in philosophy, both literally and figuratively. The principles of Confucius and the teachings of Taoism were not engraved on ivory or jade, but on humble pieces of bamboo. Bamboo manuscripts preserve the heritage of the Chinese, their intellectual culture and philosophical wisdom – a heritage that was inspired more than 2500 years ago by the symbolic strength of bamboo.

Asians have a special relationship with bamboo, the plant with a thousand and one uses. In China the appreciation for the physical qualities of bamboo went beyond their simple use, into the sphere of morality. In contrast to theoretically oriented Western philosophy, with a focus on logic and rationality, Eastern philosophies have a practical orientation and are based on intuition and tested by analogy. Because of this, bamboo is of symbolic value for human existence, in particular for understanding the essence of a good life.

What can bamboo teach us about the exemplary person? For the Chinese its deep and resilient roots stand for reliability and firmness of purpose. The long and straight stems symbolise virtuousness, the hollow interior points to modesty, and its pure exterior to chastity. Anyone who seeks to make such qualities his own is striving for perfection. Anyone who can realise such qualities in himself is exemplary. Indeed, for these reasons the philosophers and poets of China regard bamboo as the real gentleman of the forest.

Bamboo is strong and flexible, hard and soft at the same time. It is a union of opposites, reminiscent of the Yin and Yang of Taoism. Bamboo stands for strength, long life and old age, because despite long winters bamboo continues to stand straight and loses none of its leaves. It bends with the wind, and so gives way without suffering defeat. In Asia behaving 'like bamboo' means to yield and make compromises, while going on with your own life. Bamboo gets its way by giving in. The bending of bamboo is no painful retreat, but a step back, with laughter. One should not be surprised then to find that the Chinese words for bamboo and laughter are homonyms.

The flexibility of bamboo is paradigmatic for understanding social and personal relations. Confucius taught that there are five basic relationships of obligation: the relation between ruler and subject, father and son, man and wife, older brother and younger brother, and the relation between friends. According to him, men require three virtues in the practice of these relations, namely wisdom, energy and magnanimity. Some people are born with a sense of duty and the knowledge of virtue. Others obtain such knowledge by study. Still others obtain this knowledge only after a painful realisation of their ignorance. Confucius defined a guiding principle, better known as the golden rule: 'What you don't want others to do to you, you must not do to others'. The lessons that you must draw from bamboo are clear: you must have the wisdom to sway with the wind as does the bamboo. If there is drought, the bamboo preserves its energy by allowing its leaves to curl. Only when it finally rains does the bamboo return to its fantastic form. A man should likewise know how and when he must withdraw calmly in order to overcome opposition. To nobly face hardships as the bamboo does in winter, that is, standing tall, graceful and calm, is a moral ideal. If a person has the energy to persevere in this approach to other people and situations, then he will be free, as is the largest bamboo.

Luc Vermeerbergen in the National Botanical Garden of Belgium

Interiors

With increasing world-wide concern about the environment, interest in bamboo as a material to be used for interiors has undoubtedly grown in both Western Europe and
the United States. But for now bamboo design remains a
pretentious term, because it supposes a mechanised
production process. When we are dealing with bamboo this
is – leaving aside several exceptions – still hardly the case.

When they hear the term bamboo design, most people think
of the results of craftwork, where use is made of the bamboo
stem, in particular in functions where dimensional accuracy
is not of paramount importance. The production of interior
design products made of bamboo traditionally takes place in
the developing countries of Southeast Asia or South
America, but also in other countries such as China these
kinds of products tend to be exported. In almost all cases it
involves bamboo in its natural and efficient round form.

With the development of techniques that allow the manufacture of flat sheets of material from bamboo canes,

the idea of bamboo design has taken a more concrete shape.
Currently it is craftsmen who are responsible for the realisation of bamboo designs. While this does indeed involve several stages, these are rather low-key processes in which the
design can hardly be separated from the production.

Currently it is primarily people with artistic drive and ideas of
their own who design bamboo furniture. The emphasis lies
on the expressive qualities of the product – with results that
are often as surprising as they are beautiful. But in the most
design-sensitive and advanced posts of Western Europe,
a careful beginning is being made at coupling commercial
and aesthetic ideas regarding the use of bamboo.

The increasing use of bamboo for interior design can be
said to be encouraging and hopeful – especially in light of
the fact that in this new century sustainability in the purest
sense of the word must be the guide for any kind of
design. With its rapid growth and excellent qualities,
bamboo is the most logical replacement for the hard-
woods that are becoming increasingly scarce worldwide.
Bamboo is simply the better solution.

The regard for bamboo in the West has made a real turn-around in recent years. To a large extent this certainly to be explained by the excellent performances of bamboo sheet material. At the same time there have been intense efforts to understand better the properties of those bamboo species that are usable industrially. This has led to bamboo stems being introduced as building materials. Privacy screens made of bamboo are presently being used as fences around yards through entire residential neighbourhoods. They are durable, simple and beautiful. In the meantime, enthusiastic and passionate designers are busy conceiving interiors and furniture in which bamboo is the principal material. The results are dazzling and startling at the same time.

Designer with respect for the environment

'The designers of the future have to know about the working parameters of a sustainable timber for a healthy planet'

Anyone interested in bamboo is certain to know the classic bed-sofa of black bamboo, or one of the comfortable, inviting chairs by Linda Garland, either as an original design or as a copy. Research into bamboo inevitably leads to Linda Garland and the island where she works, Bali.

After she took Indonesian citizenship in 1978, Linda Garland sought a suitable place to live on the island of Bali. On the edge of the artists' village of Ubud she established the Panchoran Retreat ('panchoran' means the place where

many springs rise). The site contains five houses where people can reside as guests, and several swimming pools and quiet areas where one can read, relax and eat. In addition to many varieties of plants to admire and taste, there is a jungle-like bamboo forest with at least 200 different species of bamboo. The houses are to a great extent built of bamboo. Walls, flooring, sofas and other design elements are made from bamboo or other natural materials.

This exceptional place is a focus for creativity, research and information. With her Environmental Bamboo Foundation (EBF), established in 1993, Linda Garland strives for more familiarity with bamboo around the world, and seeks to give publicity to the new discoveries in the field of bamboo research. In 1995 the Indonesian foundation organised the 4th International Bamboo Conference on Bali (5th International Bamboo Workshop). Further, the EBF provides leadership for bamboo projects in Indonesia and many other countries around the globe, and is present at all important congresses and conferences about bamboo and environmentally friendly materials. With the EBF, Linda Garland has also developed and publicised environmentally friendly methods for combating insects that damage bamboo.

For Linda Garland, the work of the Foundation and her design activities go hand in hand. New information and studies about bamboo make the work of designers and architects all over the world easier, and assure that the plant wins more acceptance as a sustainable construction and design material.
Co-operation with young designers and architects is therefore also very important for her. The EBF functions as a forum for the exchange of information and experience. Students are given a chance here to co-operate in a future attuned to sustainable production.

Following her motto of 'designing for finding solutions for the future', Linda Garland tries to use each part of the bamboo plant for her design. The jewellery from her design collection is comprised primarily from waste products from bamboo, combined with silver.

For Linda Garland, it is above all the environmentally friendly translation of ideas and projects around the theme of bamboo that is to be focussed on. Global environmental issues that can be solved by bamboo projects have top priority for her.

Bibliography

Arun Kumar et al. *Bamboo for Sustainable Development*. 2002; ISBN 90-6764-357-2

Belcher B. et al. *Bamboo. People and the environment*. 1995; ISBN 81-86247-15-7

Bell M. *Bamboe. Gids voor liefhebbers en vakmensen*. 2000; ISBN 90-6097-548-0

Chapman G.P. *The Bamboos*. 1997; ISBN 0-12-168555-1

Crouzet Y. *Les Bambous*, 1981; ISBN 2-205-01839-6

Crouzet Y. & Jeury M. *Des Bambous dans tous les Jardins*. 1992; ISBN 2-84038-025-0

Cusack V. *Bamboo Rediscovered*. 1997; ISBN 0-9595889-8-1

Cusack V. *Bamboo World*. ISBN 0-86417-934-0

Cusack V. & Stewart D. *Bamboo World: The Growing and Use of Clumping Bamboos*. 2000; ISBN 0743200667

Dart D.L. *The Bamboo Handbook*. ISBN 0-958551405

Demoly J.P. *Bambous en France*. 1996; ISBN 2-9510511-0-7

Dicken Castro *La Guadua, un material versatil*. 1985; ISBN 958-9045-13-8

Dransfield S. *The Bamboos of Sabah*. 1992; ISBN 983-9554-03-4

Dransfield S. & Widjaja E.A. *Bamboos*. 1998; ISBN 979-8316-21-5

Eberts W. *Bamboe in huis en tuin*. ISBN 90-5210-098-5

Farrelly D. *The Book of Bamboo*. 1984; ISBN 0-87156-825-X

Fernandez E.C. & Gielis J. *Compendium of Research on Bamboo*. 2003

Freeman-Mitford A.B. *The Bamboo Garden*. 1896 (reprint 1994, American Bamboo Society)

Hamilton F. & Leopold B. *Secondary fibres and Non-Wood Pulping*. 1987; ISBN 0-919893-37-6

Hildago-Lopez O. *Bamboo, the Gift of the Gods*. 2003; ISBN 958-33-4298-X

Janssen J.J.A. *Building with Bamboo*. 1995; ISBN 1-85339-203-0

Janssen J.J.A. *Mechanical Properties of Bamboo*. 1991; ISBN 0-7923-1260-0

Jayanetti L. & Follet P. *Bamboo in Construction*. 1998; ISBN 1-900510-03-0

Jianfei Z. *Chinese Bamboos*. 1988; ISBN 0-931146-11-9

Jorge Campos Roasio et al. *Bambu in Chile*. 2003

Judziewicz E.J. et al. *American Bamboos*. 1999; ISBN 1-56098-569-0

Karki M. et al. *The Role of Bamboo. Rattan & Medicinal Plants in Mountain Development*. ISBN 81-86247-21-1

Kwaschik R. et al. *Inspirations, recipes featuring bamboo shoots*. 2003.

Leppich E. *Bambus in Kunst & Kunstgewerbe*

Lewis D. *Hardy Bamboos for Shoots and Poles*. 1998; ISBN 0966814207

Liese W. *Bamboos. Biology, silvics, properties, utilization*. 1985; ISBN 3-88085-273

Liese W. *The Anatomy of Bamboo Culms*. 1998; ISBN 81-86247-26-2

McClure F.A. *The Bamboos*. 1993; ISBN 1-56098-323-X

Meredith T.J. *Bamboo for Gardens*. 2001; ISBN 0-88192-507-1

Moore N.B. & Wein B. *Bamboo in Japan*. ISBN 4-7700-2510-6

Ohrnberger, D. *The Bamboos of the World*. 1999; ISBN 0-444-50020-0

Ohrnberger, D. & Gorrings, J. *The Bamboos of the World*. 1983-87; ISBN 81-7089-115-9

Okamura H. & Tanaka Y. *The Horticultural Bamboo Species in Japan*. 1986; ISBN 4-924764-01-9

Oprins J. & Gielis J. *Bamboe*. 1997

Planning Commission Government of India *National Mission on Bamboo Technology and Trade Development*. 2003

Ranjan M.P. et al. *Bamboo and Cane Crafts of Northeast India*. 2004; ISBN 81-86199-50-0

Recht C. & Wetterwald M.F. *Bambus*. 1988; ISBN 3-8001-6343-8

Seethalakshimi K.K. & Muktesh Kumar M.S. *Bamboos of India*. 1998; ISBN 81-86247-25-4

Shanmughavel P. et al. *Plantation Bamboo*. ISBN 81-7089-245-7

Stapleton C. *Bamboos of Nepal*. ISBN 0-947643-88-0

Stapleton C. *Bamboos of Bhutan*. ISBN 0-947643-67-2

Starosta P. & Crouzet Y. *Bamboos*. 1998; ISBN 3-8228-7759-X

Suzuki Dr. S. *Index to Japanese Bambusaceae*.

Suzuki O. & Yoshikawa I. *The Bamboo Fences of Japan*. 1988; ISBN 4-7661-0474-9

Taibei Shi *Colored Illustrations of Bambusoideae in China*. 1993

Takama S. *Die Wunderbare Welt des Bambus*. ISBN 3-7701-3800-7

van Doesburg J. & van Biemen H. *Bamboe. Een verrassende plant in uw tuin*. ISBN 90 210 0486 0

Villegas M. *New Bamboo, Architecture and Design*. 2003; ISBN 958-815606-8

Vitra Design Museum *Grow Your Own House*. ISBN 3-931936-25-2

Wang Dajun & Shen Shao-Jin *Bamboos of China*. 1987; ISBN 0-88192-074-6

Zhu Shilin et al. *A Compendium of Chinese Bamboo*. 1994

Index

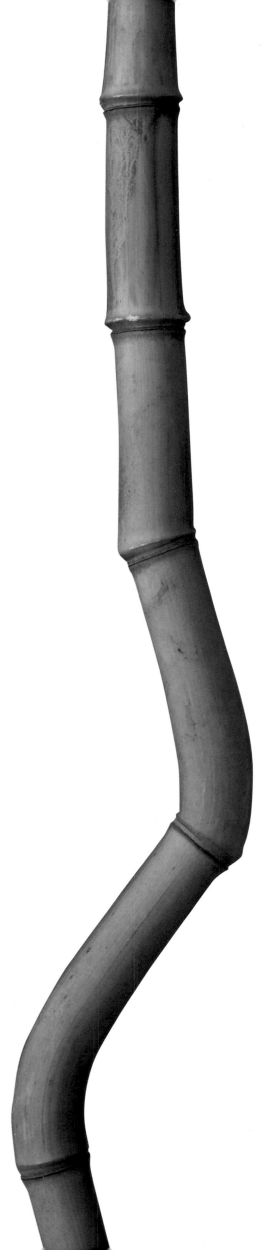

Addresses

American Bamboo Society
http://www.americanbamboo.org/

Bamboe informatie centrum Nederland
http://www.bamboe-ic.nl/

Bamboo Plantations Group
http://groups.yahoo.com/group/bamboo-plantations/

Bamboo Select
http://www.bambooselect.com

Bamboo Society of Australia
http://www.bamboo.org.au/

Bamboo Thematic Network
http://www.bamboonetwork.org

Baumschule Eberts
http://www.bambus.de/eberts/index.html

European Bamboo Society
http://www.bodley.ox.ac.uk/users/djh/ebs/ebsindex.htm

International Network for Bamboo and Rattan
http://www.inbar.int

Kimmei – Jos van der Palen
http://home.iae.nl/users/palen/kimmei.htm

La Bambouseraie de Prafrance
http://www.bambouseraie.fr/

Linda Garland
http://www.lindagarland.com

Oprins Plant
http://www.oprins.com

Reiner Winkendick – Zoo Gartenbau
http://www.winkendick.de

Rezo Plant – Frankrijk
http://www.rezo-plant.com/

World Bamboo Organization
http://www.worldbamboo.org

Environmental Bamboo Foundation
http://www.bamboocentral.org

Belgische Bamboevereniging:
BBS België
www.exoticgarden.be
www.bodley.ox.ac.uk/users/djh/ebs/ebsb.htm

Nederlandse Bamboevereniging:
EBS Nederland
 Secretariaat
 Eiland 36
 6107 CC Stevensweert
Tel: +31- 475 550755
www.bamboepagina.nl

Rice field, Yangshuo, China

Authors

Jan Oprins
Harry van Trier
Johan Gielis
Walter Liese
Suzanne Lucas
Shozo Shibata
Victor Brias
Michel Abadie
Charley Younge
Marion Lammersen / Linda Garland
Kasia J. Cwiertka
Guy Henderieckx
An Theunynck

Illustration credits

Hugo Maertens

and:
Dominique Van Huffel:
    p. 14, 16 (above right), 30, 37, 54, 59, 63 (below),
    69 (below), 88 (above), 116-117, 129
Michel Abadie:
    p. 104-107, 119
La Bambouseraie de Prafrance:
    p. 96-97
Bambus-Centrum Deutschland, Baumschule Eberts :
    p. 86-87
James Clever:
    p. 50
Guy Henderieckx:
    p. 8-9, 57, 60, 63 (above), 68, 90 (above left), 94 (above)
Marion Lammersen:
    p. 102, 132-135, 141
Bart Van Leuven:
    p. 121, 122, 123
Antonios Levissianos:
    p. 110, 111, 112, 113, 114, 115
Walter Liese:
    p. 24, 25, 26, 27, 108-109
Oprins Plant:
    p. 16 (above left + below), 21 (below left), 41 (below right)
Isabelle Persyn:
    p. 124, 125, 126, 127, 138
Irawan Prasetyo:
    p. 133 (above)
Rezo plant:
    p. 36
Luk Vermeerbergen:
    p. 128
Reiner Winkendick:
    p. 58
Charley Younge, Bamboepark Schellinkhout:
    p. 130-131

Illustration p. 2: Shorn stalks of *Phyllostachys aurea* along a
heavily used walk. Private Garden, Rijkevorsel, Belgium

Illustration p. 5: *Phyllostachys aureosulcata* 'Aureocaulis'
has splendid yellow stalks, very suitable for use as a
solitary planting

Coordination

An Theunynck, Oostkamp, Belgium

Copy editing

Femke De Lameillieure, Oostkamp, Belgium

Translation into English

Donald Mader, Rotterdam, The Netherlands

Layout, Lithography and Printing

Graphic Group Van Damme bvba, Oostkamp, Belgium

Binding

Scheerders-Van Kerchove, Sint-Niklaas, Belgium

A CIP catalogue record for this book is available from the Library
of Congress, Washington D.C., USA

Bibliographic information published by Die Deutsche Bibliothek
Die Deutsche Bibliothek lists this publication in the Deutsche
Nationalbibliografie; detailed bibliographic data is available in
the Internet at http://dnb.ddb.de.

Originally published in 2004 under the title "Bambuseae" by
Stichting Kunstboek bvba
Legeweg 165, B-8020 Oostkamp. www.stichtingkunstboek.com
© 2004 Stichting Kunstboek bvba

English Edition
© 2006 Birkhäuser – Publishers for Architecture, P.O.Box 133,
CH-4010 Basel, Switzerland
Part of Springer Science + Business Media
Printed on acid-free paper produced from chlorine-free pulp. TCF ∞
Printed in Belgium
ISBN-13 978-3-7643-7481-5
ISBN-10 3-7643-7481-0

www.birkhauser.ch

9 8 7 6 5 4 3 2 1